Allie stopped, and then turned back to Charlie, a much too innocent look on her face. "How about a small favour?"

"Smaller than sex?"

"Yes." She drifted back to him, and he felt wary again.

"What?"

Allie took off her glasses and lifted her chin. "Kiss me. So I can concentrate this time. I missed it last time. In the bar."

Charlie ran his fingers through his hair. All his instincts told him to run, but she was standing there with that great mouth, and he wanted it. "You really are something. You treat all the guys you meet like this?"

Allie shook her head, and he watched the light glint in her hair as it swung back and forth. "Nope. You just happened to hit me on a very unusual day."

"Lucky me." Charlie swallowed and surrendered. "Okay, pucker up, but this time, pay attention. I don't want to have to keep on doing this."

She nodded. "Right."

Allie lifted her face to his, and he bent and kissed her. He meant to make it brief, but the softness of her mouth moved against his and took his breath away. *I'm in big trouble here*, he thought, and then he stopped thinking.

Jennifer Crusie

Charlie
All Night

MIRA® BOOKS

*MIRA is a registered trademark of Harlequin Enterprises Limited,
used under licence.*

*First published in Great Britain in 2005.
MIRA Books, Eton House, 18-24 Paradise Road,
Richmond, Surrey, TW9 1SR*

© Jennifer Crusie 1996

ISBN 0 77830 075 6

58-0405

*Printed and bound in Spain
by Litografía Rosés S.A., Barcelona*

For Valerie Taylor,
who has the eye of an editor and the heart of a
reader, and for Brenna Todd, whose big hair is
only exceeded by her big heart, because they
got me through this book.

One

Allie McGuffey knew a yuppie bar was a lousy place to find a hero, but she was desperate, so she had to make do with what she had on hand.

Unfortunately, what she had on hand was pretty pathetic.

She shoved her horn-rimmed glasses back up the bridge of her nose with one finger and peered at the row of stools at the bar. Businessman. Businessman. Empty seat. Businessman. Businesswoman. Empty seat. Empty seat. Thug. Businessman.

She swallowed the lump that had been in her throat for the past fifteen minutes. Okay, fine, if that's what she had to work with, she'd work with it. But it was going to have to be the thug, because she was never going to have a relationship with a suit again as long as she lived. Even a relationship that was only going to last five minutes.

And he really wasn't a thug. Allie tried to drum up some enthusiasm before she made her move. His dark blond hair was shaggy over his collar, and his brown leather jacket had seen better days, and his jeans were authentic grunge, but he was big and clean and most important of all, he made a nice contrast to all the charcoal suits that looked like Mark. And what Allie wanted more than anything right then was a not-Mark.

She knew she was behaving like an idiot, but given the bomb that had just exploded in her face, the fact that she was not sitting in a trance was a step in the right direction.

It had not been a good day.

Allie had hit the radio-station doors that afternoon at her usual clip, banging them open like saloon doors. If they ever locked those doors, she was going to seriously hurt herself, but they never did since everyone had to be buzzed in from the street level four floors below. So she'd gone charging through as usual, happy to be there. As usual, what seemed like forty people converged on her.

Allie beamed as they pounced, loving the feeling that WBBB couldn't run without her, that without her there would be dead air and dust. This was who she was, Allie-the-producer, Allie-the-brains-behind-The-Mark-King-Show, Allie-the-savior. She knew she was probably a little whacked to depend on a radio station for her identity, but compared to all the other psychological problems running loose at the station, she was in relatively good mental health, so she didn't dwell on it.

At first it was just Karen, the receptionist, who called out "Allie!," but that alerted Lisa, her former student intern, who popped out of the hall looking miserable and said, "Allie, I—" and who was promptly pushed aside by Albert the financial manager, who said, "Allie, the ratings—" and who was overrun by Marcia, the two-to-six-time-slot barracuda, who said, "Allie, I heard—" and who was shouldered aside by

Mark, Allie's ex-lover and present boss, who said, "I need to see you in your office. Now."

Allie pushed her glasses back up her nose so she could see him better. The silence that settled over the reception area was a tribute to how bizarrely Mark was behaving. Usually, he made his presence known through talking too loudly, dropping names and laughing heartily in the wrong places. Allie had once felt sorry for him, but she didn't now, having been dumped as his lover two months ago when he decided he'd look better standing next to Lisa than he did with her. He was right, of course, but it still hurt to look at him now. He stood in the entrance to the hallway, quietly superior, and it was such a change that everybody shut up and she followed him to her office without question.

Once inside, he closed the door behind her, went around to her desk chair and sat.

Allie fought back a snarl. All right, she wasn't territorial, but this was her office, no matter how tiny and cluttered, and her desk, and that was her desk chair, and he was making her a visitor in her own domain. So she scowled at him and said, "What is this?"

Mark crossed his arms and leaned back in her chair, which tilted so that he was almost horizontal to her vertical, and then he said, "There's no good way to tell you this, Allie, so I'll just say it. I know it's going to be hard, but I also know you're an adult and you realize that things change. People grow. Change is good." He let his head fall back and addressed the ceiling as he began to wax philosophic. While Allie waited for him to get to the point, assuming he had one, she considered how amazingly good-looking he was, and how mad she was at him, and how much she wanted him back.

This was the great mystery of her life. He was an insecure twit. So why had she fallen for him and why was she still hung up on him? Why did she miss going to dinner with him and lying in bed with him, all the while listening to him talk about himself? Of course, that had been research for the show, but still... As he droned on and she automatically began to edit his speech for broadcast purposes, the possibility dawned on her that what she'd fallen for was the edited Mark King she'd created on the radio, not the real Mark King who sat in front of her now, boring her to tears. And that what she was most mad about was that she'd created him, and then he'd taken her work to another woman.

Mark was still waxing. "So that's why—"

Allie cut in, more exasperated with herself than with Mark. "Look, I've got things to do here, so if you'll just cut to the chase, I'll get back to keeping you a hit." Okay, that was below the belt, but he'd started the fight by sitting in her chair, the louse. Not to mention dumping her for a younger woman.

Mark sat up straight and put his palms flat on her desk. "All right, here it is. You're not going to be working on my show anymore."

The room spun. Allie dropped into the remaining chair in the room and said, "What?"

"I've sensed a certain hostility since our breakup, and it's affecting my performance. So Bill and I have decided it's best to put Lisa in your place since you've trained her. That way, the show won't suffer at all."

Allie sat stunned.

Mark smiled at her and spread his hands, fait accompli. "Lisa is producing the show, starting now. It'll be better for all of us."

"All of us who?" She took a deep breath. "Not all of us me. You have the drive-time show. I'm the drive-time producer. Unless I get the slot while you and Lisa move someplace cozy, this is not better for me."

"Well, of course I'm not moving." Mark sat up straighter in the chair. "I'm the talent."

He was the talent? Then what was she?

"And you're not fired or anything like that. We do appreciate what you've done," he went on, and Allie jerked her head up, anger finally evicting her panic.

"Of course I'm not fired. Why would I be fired? This makes no sense."

He plowed on through her anger. "And Bill's going to give you another show to produce. I made sure of that."

Good old Mark. Taking care of her. What a pal. She stood up, refraining from killing him where he sat only by Herculean effort. "Well, gee, Mark, thanks for the support and good luck in the future. Now get out of my chair."

He stood, doing what she'd said as if by instinct. After two years of doing everything she said, it was probably a hard habit to break. He moved toward the door, brimming with patronizing goodwill. "Look, why don't we go out for a drink? Just to show there are no hard feelings."

She wanted to scream at him, *Of course, there are hard feelings, you jerk. If I could, I'd beat you sense-*

less with one right now. But she was too adult for that, and too rattled, so she lied instead. Mark might have kicked her in the teeth, but she still had her incisors.

"Sorry, I've already got a date. In fact, I have to go now. Maybe some other time." She ducked out into the hall in front of him, trying not to cry. That would be a real mistake because she never cried. If she did, people would probably assume somebody had died. And then she'd have to tell them that, tragically, Mark still lived.

Mark followed her, so she speeded up.

Karen yelled "Allie" again as she went past the receptionist's counter, and this time shoved an envelope at her. "Bill—"

Allie took the envelope without slowing down, flashing the best smile she could under the circumstances, and bolted for the elevator with Mark still in pursuit.

Then Karen called out to him, too, and stopped him, and Allie caught the elevator and escaped to the street.

She'd been fired. She still had a job, but her career was gone with Mark. Allie stuck her chin out and tried to fake defiance—well, big deal, she'd just build another great show—but it was no good. She'd spent two years making Mark's show a hit, taking surveys, researching topics, devising contests, doing everything she knew to showcase Mark's strengths. She'd majored in Mark King, and now he'd expelled her.

For a moment, outside the restaurant across from the station, Allie felt a moment of pure fear. What if she couldn't do it again? What if Mark was right and he was the talent? What if she really was a loser? Nobody coming to her for help, nobody relying on her.

No. She'd find a way back. She gritted her teeth and went into the restaurant.

The hallway divided the restaurant from the bar, a sort of DMZ that separated the eating yuppies from the drinking yuppies. Allie stopped there and opened the envelope Karen had thrust at her. She found the kind of note the station owner was famous for: short, tactless and to the point:

> I'm taking you off Mark's show and giving you to Charles Tenniel, the man taking over for Waldo Hancock. Meet him tomorrow, Tuesday, five o'clock, my office.
> Bill

Weird Waldo had the 10:00 to 2:00 a.m. spot. She'd just been demoted from producing the radio equivalent of *Oprah* to the radio equivalent of an infomercial.

She shoved the note back into the envelope and looked around the hallway. Her roommate Joe who was supposed to meet her wasn't there to comfort her. The hell with it. She was going home.

She turned around to go back into the street, but outside the door was Mark, greeting people who greeted him back as if he were a celebrity. Which, of course, he was.

And he was going to come into the bar and find her alone after her big talk about a date because Joe was late again. Not that Joe would have been very impressive as a date, but he would have been more impressive than no date at all.

So she went into the bar to find a date, and there

were all those suits and the thug. She couldn't face another suit, and at least the thug looked like a change of pace, so she went over to the thug and said, "Hi!" as vivaciously as she could. She wasn't vivacious by nature, so she sounded as if she'd been sucking helium, but he turned and looked at her anyway.

Allie didn't know what she'd been expecting. Maybe some fantasy guy who was even better-looking than Mark, which, in all fairness to Mark, would be impossible, but this guy wasn't even in the running. He had the kind of face that the big, good-natured kids in the back of high-school English classes always have, slightly dopey and comfortable.

He looked nice. That was about it, but after Mark, it was pretty good.

Allie plopped her bag down on the bar. "So! You meeting someone?" she asked, still on helium, and looked over her shoulder to check on the Mark situation. All she had to do was keep the thug in conversation until Mark walked in, saw she was with him and left.

Mark didn't like competition.

"So, are you?" Allie smiled like a telemarketer. "Meeting someone?" She sat down beside him, praying Mark wouldn't come in.

And he said, "No. What are you doing?"

SHORTLY BEFORE Allie picked him up, Charlie had been contemplating his future. It looked complicated and possibly dangerous, so his best plan was to lay low, not make waves, do the job and get out. Investigating the source of an incriminating anonymous letter to a radio station in Tuttle, Ohio, couldn't be that hard. The station wasn't that big. Hell, the *town* wasn't that big. His biggest problem was going to be pretending to be a disc jockey, and how hard could that be? If his brother had done it stoned, he could certainly do it straight. And he'd made it clear to everybody concerned that he was only around for six weeks, tops. He had things to do, he'd told them, places he had to be in November.

He hadn't decided yet exactly what place he had to be in November, but he was positive it was somewhere uncomplicated and remote. Especially remote from his father who had taken to asking weird favors lately. Like "Check into this radio station for my old friend Bill..." This was what came of going home for his father's birthday. From now on, he'd just send a card. And as soon as he was done, he was out of here and someplace else. Someplace where he could do something simple for a while, like raise pigs. No, too complicated. He'd raise carrots. You didn't have to feed carrots.

He'd stopped thinking when somebody had squeaked, "Hi!"

Charlie had blinked at her, mildly surprised. She didn't look like the vivacious pick-up-a-guy-in-a-bar type. Her sharp brown eyes gleamed behind huge, round, horn-rimmed glasses, and her glossy gold-brown hair swung in a tangled Dutch-boy bob. There was nothing wrong with her nose or mouth, either; good standard-issue all-American-woman features. She just seemed sort of scrubbed to be trolling for guys. The long flowered skirt and oversize vest weren't right for a pickup, either. She looked like a nice, clean kid. Well, she was no kid. Early thirties easy.

She raised her eyebrows so high they disappeared under her bangs and batted her eyelashes. "So! You meeting someone?" She looked over her shoulder and flopped her bag down on the bar. It looked as if it was made from very old blue flowered carpet. Charlie had never seen anything quite like it so he poked his finger into it. It was fuzzy.

"Are you?" She smiled at him again, a sort of strained, too-many-teeth, trying-too-hard smile. "Meeting someone?" She sat on the stool beside him.

"No." Charlie looked at her with interest. "What are you doing?"

"Picking you up?"

Charlie shook his head. "I don't think so. What are you really doing?"

The artificial smile morphed into a genuine scowl, and her perky voice dropped an octave. "I don't believe this. Can't you even pretend on the hope you'll get lucky?"

"I never pretend. I'm the natural, open type." Charlie considered moving away from her and then rejected the idea. If he left her, he'd never find out what she was up to. And besides, when she'd scowled at him, her voice had gone husky. She had a great low voice. He smiled down at her, trying to make her talk again. "Why don't you just give me the drift, and then we can take it from there."

She lowered her head a little and stared at him over the rims of her glasses. "Look, the drift will take too long, and besides, it makes me look pathetic. All I ask is that you pretend to be having a drink with me." He must have looked skeptical because she added, "I swear that's it."

Right. Charlie had been wandering through the world long enough to know that wouldn't be it, that there would be complications. There were always complications, which was why Charlie had spent his thirty-four years learning to be light on his feet and fast out the door.

On the other hand, she wasn't part of his current problem so there weren't likely to be long-term complications. He had a free evening before he had to go poking around in other people's business, so he might as well poke around in hers for a while. At the very least, he'd get to listen to her talk. He shrugged. "Hell, it's worth one drink just to find out what happens next." He motioned to the bartender.

"I'm quite sure he won't come over here." She looked back over her shoulder again.

The bartender came and Charlie said, "The lady would like…" He turned back to her.

"The lady would like to pay for her own amaretto and cream, Max." She took a couple of bills out of her carpet bag and handed them to the bartender as she looked over her shoulder again.

"You got it, Allie," the bartender said and moved away.

"Amaretto and cream?" Charlie frowned. "That's disgusting."

"At least the cream part is good for me." She turned back to him. "Well, it should be skim milk, but bars never have skim milk."

"That's true." Charlie drew back a little. "You

know, you have the weirdest pickup line in North America.''

"Pickup line?" She swiveled on the stool and faced him. Her eyes sparked at him and her cheeks glowed rosy with outrage. Outrage looked very good on her. "This isn't a pickup line. The pickup line was before, the one that didn't work." She swiveled again to keep lookout. "Oh, great." She swiveled to face him again. "There he is. Okay, here's the deal. We're together. Try to look like you haven't just insulted me."

"I didn't insult you. I made an observation."

"Well, stop." She looked back over her shoulder again. "Oh, no." She closed her eyes. Charlie saw her lips moving and leaned closer to hear her, but she wasn't talking to him. "He's going to go by. I'm sure he's going to go by. I'm sure…"

A male-model type stopped on the other side of her. "Allie! There you are. I—"

She jerked as if she'd been shot. "Mark! What a surprise. To see you. Again. So soon." She looked at Charlie and said, very softly, "Oh, hell."

Then she stuck her chin out and turned to smile at Mark.

She was doing pretty good, Charlie thought. Good smile. Pretty lame answer, but the smile and the chin would probably make up for it. He looked at the guy. Tall, dark and handsome, if you liked really pretty men. Very expensive suit. Toothpaste grin. And the jerk was smiling that grin at her as if he knew she was in agony. Charlie shook his head at the situation and finished his drink. Good thing he wasn't involved in this one. It was a mess.

"Let me buy you a drink, Al. It's the least I can do." Mark the jerk motioned for the bartender.

Max wandered back and put Allie's amaretto in front of her.

"No, no." Allie's mouth went lipless with stress. "I have one. Thanks, Max."

"Amaretto and cream." Mark laughed. "Good old Allie." He sat down beside her at the bar and patted her on the back.

"Grrrrr." It was a very faint low growl, locked behind her teeth, almost indiscernible in the babble of the bar, but Charlie heard it because she'd turned to him as she made it. "I'm sorry about this," Allie whispered to him.

Charlie leaned forward and whispered in her ear, "Try not to look like a wounded basset hound."

Allie flashed Mark a brilliant smile over her shoulder.

"I didn't realize the two of you were together." Mark paused for an introduction.

Allie kept on smiling like a half-wit, so Charlie took pity on her and extended his hand past her nose. "Charlie Tenniel."

Allie started, but Mark took his hand with enthusiasm, gripping it in a he-man clasp. Charlie let his hand go limp. Mark smirked.

What an idiot, Charlie thought.

Mark was positively jovial. "Well, this is a coincidence. I'm Mark King. You've inherited my producer, you lucky dog. I've taught her everything there is to know about radio. You're in good hands."

Allie made that low growling sound in her throat again, and Charlie blinked at them both and then let

Mark babble on about his own many successes, ignoring him for heavier thoughts. So much for diverting himself with Allie. Allie worked at the station with Mark the jerk. They were probably both in trouble up to their necks.

Allie certainly looked as if she was in trouble. She turned bleak, questioning eyes on him. "Is this true?" she whispered. "You're my new DJ?" He nodded at her and she closed her eyes. "We were just discussing that," she lied as she turned back to Mark.

Charlie picked up her glass of cream and handed it to her. "Here you go, boss. Glad to meet you, Mark. This the place everybody at the station hangs out?"

"Pretty much. Convenient. Right across the street, you know." Mark smiled broadly while he sized Charlie up with obvious confidence. "Have you two known each other long?"

Allie put down her newly empty glass. "Oh, it seems like it."

Charlie brought his mind back to the problem at hand. "Don't chug cream like that." He took the empty glass from her. "This isn't skim milk, you know. This is the real thing, the hard stuff. Max, another amaretto and cream for the lady. In fact, just bring over the bottle and drive in the cow."

"A comedian." Allie nodded her head. "Five guys sitting at a bar, and I pick the comedian."

"What?" Mark leaned closer to catch what she was saying.

"She thinks I'm funny." Charlie put his arm around Allie and gave her an affectionate squeeze. She was a lot softer than he was prepared for, so he left his arm where it was for a while. "Funny is the basis for any good relationship."

"Maybe that's what was wrong with us, huh, Allie?" Mark looked soulfully at her.

What a goof.

"You two were once…" Charlie wiggled his eyebrows at Allie. "You never told me that."

"It never came up." Allie glared at him from the curve of his arm.

"You're a lucky man, Tenniel." Mark was still trying to recapture Allie's attention, but she missed his meaningful looks because she was busy glaring at Charlie.

Charlie beamed at them both, enjoying the situation. "That's what everybody keeps telling me. Actually, it's not luck, it's skill."

Mark tried again. "So how did you two meet?"

"In a bar," Charlie said. "She picked me up."

"Allie did?" Mark looked astounded.

"She begged me to buy her a drink."

"Allie did?"

Charlie nodded. "Happens to me all the time. Animal magnetism."

"Oh, a joke." Mark looked relieved. "How did you two really meet?"

"I picked him up." Allie took a deep breath. "The truth is…"

Charlie pulled her tighter, momentarily shutting down her lungs. "The truth is, she sat down next to me, and I looked at her and thought, 'This is a good-looking woman,' and we started to talk, and we've been together ever since."

Allie jerked her head up and stared at him. Then

she smiled, and Charlie smiled back by reflex, caught by the intelligence in her eyes and the warmth in her wide, soft mouth. She leaned toward him, and he bent to hear what she said.

She was almost nose to nose with him. "You are a good person. I forgive you for insulting me." She patted his sleeve and then disengaged herself from his arm.

Charlie missed her warmth. "I didn't insult you."

"How long have you two known each other?" Mark asked.

"Eternity," Charlie said.

"But it seems like only a few short minutes." Allie glared at him again and then she leaned back, her attention caught by something over Charlie's shoulder. She signaled someone away, and Charlie turned just in time to get the impression that someone was doing a fade from the doorway into the hall.

So, Allie had a secret. Life just got more interesting all the time. And of course that meant that he was going to have to stick with her until he discovered her secret. He'd been hired to find all the secrets at the station. It was his job. It was his duty. He looked at Allie, her hair shining like old brass in the warm light of the bar.

It was his pleasure.

"So, where's Lisa tonight?" Allie leaned on the bar in an attempt at languid unconcern. "What a shame she's not with you. We could all have dinner together."

Careful, Allie, Charlie thought.

"Lisa's at the station." Mark frowned. "You're

right. It is a shame. This would be a great chance to meet Charlie.''

''There'll be other chances.'' Charlie finished his drink. ''I'm not going anyplace. Except to the top of the ratings.''

Mark decided that was a joke, too. ''Heh, heh, heh.''

Mark had a laugh like an asthmatic horse, and Charlie wondered if that was why Allie had left him. Listening to that laugh would certainly be reason enough for anybody to leave him. Which brought an ugly thought. He'd have to be very careful because if Mark was any indication of his radio competition, he *would* go to the top of the ratings. That would be bad. One of the basic tenets of undercover investigation was not becoming a household word.

''Well!'' Allie slid off the stool. ''We've got to be getting in to dinner. Wonderful seeing you again, Mark.''

Mark leaned forward to kiss her goodbye, and she tripped backward to get away from him.

Charlie caught her. ''Falling for me all over again, huh?'' He tightened his arm around her automatically. Allie was soft and round against his shoulder, and she smelled like flowers. He was in no hurry to let go. ''Try to restrain yourself,'' he told her. ''We're in public.''

She looked into his eyes and swallowed hard. ''It's your animal magnetism. I'm restrained now. You can let go.''

''I don't think so,'' he said, and kissed her.

He'd only meant to kiss her quickly and let her go, mostly to annoy Mark and, all right, because she had

a great mouth. But she clutched at him in surprise and
fell into his arms so the kiss was a lot more than he'd
planned, a lot more warmth and softness and weight,
and her mouth was cool and sweet from the cream.
He was a little dizzy by the time he remembered where
he was and came up for air.

"What are you doing?" Allie sounded more breathless than annoyed when she pulled away from him.

"Making my move. Come back here." Charlie
reached for her, and she stepped back.

Mark looked disgruntled. "Well, really, Allie,
you're in public."

"That's lust." Charlie smiled at him happily. "She
can't keep her lips off me." Allie took another step
back, and Charlie stood up to follow her. "Well, it
looks like we're moving on," he told Mark. "Tell Lisa
we said hi."

When they were in the hallway, Allie shook her
head. "Who are you really? Satan? I'm being pun-
ished, right?"

"I'm Charlie Tenniel." He held out his hand. "I
work with that stuffed shirt you used to date. I assume
all you did was date. I'd hate to think that any woman
I'd kissed in a bar actually went to bed with somebody
like that."

She looked down at his hand and sighed. Then she
took it and shook it once and dropped it. "I'm Alice
McGuffey, your producer at WBBB. It was nice meeting you, and thank you very much for helping me with
Mark, but I have to go now. We can talk again tomorrow at the station."

She turned to go into the restaurant, and Charlie
stepped around her to block her. The last thing he

wanted now was to get dumped. There were too many things Allie could tell him about the station. He could probably get the information from other people, but other people didn't have Allie's voice. Or Allie's mouth. "Where are you going?"

"To dinner." Allie gestured to the dining room. "With my dinner date. The only perfect man I know."

"Ah." Charlie nodded at her encouragingly. "Your father. We should meet so he can see the kind of guy you're working with."

"No."

"No, he shouldn't see?"

"No, he's not my father."

"No?" Charlie thought faster. "Gee, I've never met a perfect man." He tried to look wistful. "I've always wanted a role model."

Allie looked at him with disapproval, but he smiled at her and finally she gave up. "Okay, I owe you. You want to eat dinner with Joe and me? If you can't, it's perfectly all right."

"Thank you." Charlie held the door to the restaurant open. "I can't wait to meet Joe, the perfect man."

"Terrific," Allie said.

Charlie followed her into the restaurant, a big room with too much mahogany and not enough light. Allie looked around the dimness and then smiled when a man across the room stood up and waved at her.

Charlie narrowed his eyes a little. This guy might actually be the perfect man. He was tall, even taller than Charlie's six-two, and classically handsome without being obnoxious about it. His jaw was strong, his blond hair gleamed, his blue eyes were warm and the smile he had for Allie was real and loving.

"Your brother?" Charlie asked, and Allie said, "No," and walked away from him. He followed her, trying to find something about Joe that wasn't perfect and feeling vaguely annoyed.

Allie introduced them at the table. "Joe, this is Charlie Tenniel, the new ten-to-two DJ. I'm producing his show."

"I heard. Karen called." Joe shot Allie a look that appeared to be sympathy, but Allie had already turned back to Charlie. "Charlie, this is Joe Ericson, my roommate. He's the station's accountant."

She sounded like a well-behaved child, but she didn't look like one. Charlie began to wonder what Allie was like when she wasn't behaving well in public. *No.* That sort of thought would add those complications he'd been avoiding.

"Charlie Tenniel." Joe's smile was open and admiring as he held out his hand. "Are you the one they call Ten Tenniel?"

Ouch. He hated lying, but it was better than "No, that's my brother, the drug-dealing DJ." He shook his head. "Call me Charlie."

Joe kept going. "I've heard about you. I've got a friend down in Lawrenceville who was very upset when you disappeared. I'm looking forward to hearing you myself now."

His smile was genuine, and Charlie liked him.

"Who in Lawrenceville?" Allie had already seated herself and picked up the menu. "I'm starving."

Joe sat down next to her. "Rona. Remember? From that seminar we took?"

Charlie took the chair across from her so he could watch her.

"Right. You kept in touch with Rona?" Allie ran her finger down the menu list. "Pasta."

"I keep in touch with everybody." Joe tapped Allie's menu. "Not pasta. I'll do pasta tomorrow night. Get something here that's a pain in the butt to make. You like pasta, Charlie?"

Charlie started. Joe and Allie were so in sync in their conversation, he was a little surprised to be suddenly included. "Yep."

"Come to dinner tomorrow night."

Charlie beamed his best smile at him. "Thanks." Another contact at the station. First Allie, then Mark, now Joe. And he'd only been in town a couple of hours. God, he was good.

Allie glared at Joe.

Joe mock-glared back. "Don't look at me like that. I want to get to know Ten Tenniel."

"Charlie," Charlie said. "Just call me Charlie."

ALLIE WASN'T SURE how she felt about Charlie. He'd done a nice job of saving her from Mark, but he'd laughed the whole time he was doing it, which made her feel like a dweeb. Of course, he had a point: panic was not a good look for her. *Don't do that again,* she told herself and turned back to the problem at hand.

She now had to work with a guy who'd kissed her in a bar. This was not a good way to start a professional relationship, especially since he was quite a good kisser. It would be hard to say no if he ever suggested they try that again, and of course she'd have to say no because sleeping with the talent was not a good idea. Look what had happened with Mark. No, forget about Mark. Socializing with Charlie was not a good idea, which was why she'd tried to look quelling when he suggested he eat with Joe and her, but Charlie didn't quell easily. In fact, Charlie didn't quell at all.

He did seem taken aback when he saw Joe for the first time. Allie considered her roommate as she sat beside him. Part of Joe's impact came from the fact that he was such a good man, so everything he was sort of infused his face, and his face was perfect, so people just felt good just looking at him. She felt good just looking at him now. She'd talk this whole job mess out with him later, and everything would make sense.

But Joe did have his faults. Food, for instance.

He'd picked up his menu and was studying it as if there'd be a quiz at the end of the meal, which actually there would be. He'd ask, "Too much oregano. And where was the basil? Obvious seasoning. Sure sign of a clumsy chef. What about the asparagus?" He could go for days on just a side dish. But for right now, all he did was gesture at the menu and ask, "What do you think?"

Allie prepared for the usual battle. She was still nauseated from the stress of the afternoon, so a large slab of dead animal did not appeal. But she had to eat or she'd pass out, and she had to choose something that Joe hated to make, or he'd be insulted. "Manicotti," she decided. "The last time you made that, you bitched about stuffing all that pasta."

"Not manicotti. Mine's better than here. Get a steak."

"I don't want a steak. I want pasta."

"Well, don't come home tomorrow and say, 'Pasta? We just *had* pasta.'"

Charlie looked from one to the other. "You guys been together long?"

Allie laughed at the annoyance in his voice. "You sound just like Mark."

"Yeah, and speaking of Mark, what was that?" Joe frowned at her. "You and Mark having a drink together after he fired you?"

"Yeah." Charlie frowned at her, too. "What was that? I was there, and I didn't understand it."

Allie slumped back in her chair, her lousy day returning in full force. "That was my worst nightmare. That's why I picked up Charlie. I didn't want Mark to think I still...you know."

"We know." Joe looked at Charlie. "She's usually not this wimpy. In fact, she's usually very confident. It's just Mark that makes her act like she's twelve again."

Charlie nodded. "You should have been at the bar. She was practically incoherent."

"I was not." Allie stuck out her chin and tried to look strong and defiant, and Charlie snorted. She gave up then and dropped her head into her hands. "Oh, hell."

Joe patted her head. "There, there. You have me."

"Oh, good," Allie said without raising her head. "That's a comfort."

"Now order," Joe said. "And don't screw up."

Allie finally got Joe to agree that she could have the chicken fettuccini since he wanted a taste of it himself. Chickens weren't really dead animals, she reasoned, ready to contemplate anything except her future. They were more like protein with feathers. Joe and Charlie ordered prime rib, and Joe gave the waitress lavish instructions on their side dishes, which she copied down word for word, having served him before. When the waitress was gone, Joe remembered that he hadn't designed Allie's vegetables, and Allie argued that she wanted hers plain, and he said that was no way to live, and they were off on one of their usual arguments with lots of laughing, when Charlie interrupted.

"So, how long *have* you known each other?"

"Four years," Joe said. "Ever since she came to the station."

Allie relaxed and smiled at Joe. "I was new in town and didn't have a place to live, and he was at the station picking up the books, and his roommate had just moved out, so he said I could borrow the spare bedroom until I found a place."

Joe grinned. "And then she came home with me, and we talked and laughed until two in the morning, and I said, 'Don't find another place,' and we've been together ever since."

Charlie looked from Joe to Allie, and he didn't look happy. Allie stopped smiling, wondering what she'd said that was wrong, not really caring as long as it wasn't another major trauma to deal with. Then Charlie said, "I don't get this. If Joe is the perfect man, why did you ever get mixed up with that clown, Mark?"

Joe blinked at him. "I'm the perfect man?"

"That's what Allie says."

Joe raised his eyebrows at her. "I'm flattered."

Allied tensed. "Well, almost." She shot a look at Charlie, prepared to jettison him permanently if he said the wrong thing.

Joe looked at Charlie. "I'm gay."

Charlie relaxed and beamed at him in what looked like relief. He picked up a bread stick. "Good for you, but that doesn't justify Mark. There must be other men in this town almost as perfect as you who like girls."

Allie blinked at him. She had obviously missed something there, but since it wasn't homophobia, she didn't care what was going on in Charlie's brain. It was a male brain. It was probably incomprehensible, anyway. Look at Mark.

Joe sat back. "I've got to admit, I wasn't happy about Mark, either." He turned to Allie. "Why did you pick him?"

"I didn't." Allie tried to look unconcerned. "He picked me. I don't know why."

"I don't, either," Joe said. "You're not his type."

"What is his type?" Charlie asked.

"Lisa." Allie stuck out her chin in defiant unconcern, but unfortunately, she stuck her lower lip out farther.

"Don't pout." Joe bit into a bread stick.

"You owe Lisa, whoever she is," Charlie told her. "She saved you from a man worse than death. You say thank you very much the next time you see her."

"Which should be any minute now." Joe pointed his bread stick behind Charlie. "That's them by the door."

Allie looked up in time to see Mark wave and take Lisa's hand and tow her toward them through the crowd.

The day from hell would never end. Well, she'd asked for it.

Charlie evidently thought so, too. "It's a shame

Lisa's not with you," he mimicked. "We could all have dinner together."

"I know." Allie pushed her glasses back up the bridge of her nose and steeled herself for the mess to come. "I know. If I'd behaved like an adult, I wouldn't have picked up Charlie in a bar and lied to Mark. I deserve this."

"Nobody deserves this." Joe handed her a bread stick. "Eat. I'm with you. We can take them."

"Hell, yes." Charlie relented and patted her hand. "The odds are in our favor."

"You in this, too? Good." Joe handed him a bread stick, too. "We can always use another foot soldier in the fight against yuppie scum dweebs."

"That bad?"

"Lisa! Mark!" Joe stood up. "I was just telling Charlie all about you."

Someday, Allie told herself, _I'll look back on this and laugh._

But not yet.

Two

Allie sat numbly while Mark beamed at all of them. "Isn't this terrific. Can we join you?" He pulled out a chair for Lisa without waiting for an answer, and Lisa sat, giving Allie a cautious look under her lashes.

She had beautiful lashes. Actually, Lisa had beautiful everything. No wonder Mark had wanted her instead. There was no point in hating younger, more attractive women just because they existed. You had to wait until they did something to you to hate them. And Lisa hadn't fired her, Mark had.

Allie gave up and smiled at her. "Hi, Lisa. Congratulations on your promotion."

Lisa leaned forward, caution gone, her words tumbling out in her happiness. "It's so exciting, Allie. I can't thank you enough. Mark told me it was your decision—"

Allie's eyebrows almost hit the ceiling. "Oh?"

Lisa stopped. "It wasn't?"

Allie looked at Mark as if he were fish bait. "I'm really looking forward to working with Charlie," she lied. "Have you met Charlie yet, Lisa? Charlie Tenniel, Lisa Mitchell."

Charlie smiled at her and took her hand. "Nice to meet you."

Lisa smiled back, using her lashes on Charlie this time. "Welcome to the station. You're going to *love* working with Allie. She's—"

"So." Mark broke into the conversation loudly, and Lisa jerked her hand back. "Where are you staying, Charlie?"

Charlie leaned back a little. "I just got into town today."

Mark narrowed his eyes at Allie. "You haven't found him a place to live? That's not like you. You organize everybody."

What's your problem? Allie thought. *Jealousy? Good.* "He's staying with us," she said, and Joe choked on his drink.

"What's wrong with you?" Mark asked him.

"Nothing." Joe smiled blandly. "Nothing."

Mark frowned again at Allie. "You've only got two bedrooms."

"Yes, I know." It wouldn't hurt Mark to think she was sleeping with Charlie. She looked at Charlie over the top of her glasses. Actually, it wouldn't hurt her to think she was sleeping with Charlie. Bulky, friendly Charlie in shirtsleeves made a nice contrast to trim, tense Mark in a suit. In fact, the more she saw Mark next to Charlie, the less she missed having him around. Sleeping with Charlie might be the logical cure for her lingering case of Mark. Sort of like using penicillin to wipe out a bad bug that wouldn't go away.

The analogy was certainly apt anyway.

Allie's logic kicked into gear. She wasn't infatuated with Charlie the way she'd been with Mark. With Charlie, she could have an intelligent, well-planned one-night stand. Then her last sexual memory would be Charlie, not Mark, and she could get on with her life. The more she thought about it, the better she liked it. As long as Charlie didn't get hung up on her, it would be perfect. And even in her short acquaintance with him, it was fairly evident that commitment was not his byword.

Mark looked from Charlie to Allie to Joe, evidently reading Allie's mind. "So who is he sleeping with?"

"Me." Allie held up her hand like a polite child, her plan now in place. "Joe gets him tomorrow."

"Very funny," Mark said.

"Not so funny for me," Joe said. "I have to wait twenty-four hours."

"I don't think that's funny," Mark said.

"Neither does Joe," Charlie said, and Allie laughed, delighted he was part of them.

Lisa had been following the exchange, frowning as her head bobbed back and forth. "I don't get it."

"It's just a joke, Lisa." Mark put his arm around her. "Not a very funny one."

Charlie shook his head. "You have no sense of humor, Mark. That's why your relationship with Allie didn't work, remember?"

Mark decided to take offense, something, Allie reflected, that any sane man would have taken much sooner. "I don't know what Allie is doing with someone like you," Mark told Charlie. "You're not her type. Of course, I don't know what she's doing with *him*, either." He jerked his head at Joe.

Allie did not take insults to any of her friends well, but especially not to Joe. *"Look…"*

"I'm great in the kitchen," Joe said. "She loves my cooking."

"And I'm great in the bedroom," Charlie said. "She loves my body. Between the two of us, Allie has it all."

Allie glared at them both. "Actually—"

Mark snorted. "Allie doesn't like sex."

Allie swung on Mark. "Well, *actually*—"

Charlie smiled at Mark. "No, she just didn't like it with you."

"She didn't like your linguini, either," Joe pointed out. "She said it was rubbery."

Charlie frowned at Joe. "That's funny. She said the same thing about his—"

"Oh, *great*," Allie said.

"Don't be childish." Mark stood up, almost knocking over the waitress who'd come with their salads. "Obviously, we've intruded, and you don't want us. Come on, Lisa."

They watched him stalk across the room, Lisa trailing behind, throwing them curious looks over her shoulder.

"Feel free to discuss my sex life at any time in public," Allie told the two of them when the waitress had gone. "Don't mind me."

"We won't," Charlie said around a mouthful of salad.

"I almost feel sorry for Lisa," Joe said.

Allie picked up her fork and stabbed at her lettuce, shoving thoughts of sleeping with Charlie out of her mind to consider Lisa. She ate for a couple of minutes, looking at the situation from all sides. "I guess I do feel sorry for her," she said finally. "This isn't her fault."

"She ended up with your boyfriend and your job,"

Joe reminded her. "She has some responsibility there."

"Nope." Allie's voice grew firmer as she grew surer. "This is Mark. Mark wanted me out and her in. And he got it. I just don't know why."

Joe shook his head at her. "It's obvious. Mark's jealous of you."

"That makes no sense." Allie waved her fork at him to end the discussion.

"Yeah, it does." Joe pointed his own fork at her. "Everybody at the station knows that Mark's success is because of you. He likes to think it's because of him."

Charlie stabbed another chunk of lettuce. "So, if he shoves Allie out and puts Lisa the newbie in, everyone will know that his success is—"

"His success," Joe finished. "Except that's not going to happen."

"Why not?" Charlie shoved his empty salad bowl aside and reached for another bread stick.

"You eat like you're starving," Allie told him, amazed at the speed with which he'd destroyed his salad. "Don't they feed you back home?"

"You should talk." He pointed to her own half-empty bowl. "I've seen locusts move through vegetation slower." He turned back to Joe. "Why not?"

Joe scooped up a forkful of his salad. "Because the only reason Mark is a success is because Allie plans out every second of his show. She even has his ad-libs on cue cards. You have to see it to believe it."

Charlie raised an eyebrow at Allie. "How do you manage that?"

Allie shrugged. "There are only a dozen or so expressions that are really useful, anyway. I just pick the card that worked best. And he isn't that bad. In almost two years, he's never misread a cue card. Could we talk about something else?''

''Oh, that's talent, reading cue cards,'' Charlie agreed. ''You were with him for two years?''

''Professionally.'' Allie squirmed a little in her chair. ''The other thing only lasted about six months.''

''Six terrible months,'' Joe added. ''Thank God for Lisa, or I'd have had to kill him just to set you free. And you're right, Al, I do feel sorry for her. She's going to pay.''

Charlie looked around the table for something else to eat. ''Why? What did she do now?''

''Nothing.'' Joe grinned at him over his salad bowl. ''Do you remember the flack Deborah Norville got when she replaced Jane Pauley?''

''Yeah.'' Charlie fished a pepper strip out of Allie's bowl, narrowly avoiding her fork.

''Well, that's going to be nothing compared to what happens when the station finds out Allie got screwed. Lisa is not going to have an easy time of it.''

Allie was afraid for a moment that Joe might have a point. She didn't mind Lisa failing to keep Mark's ratings up, but she didn't want her to fail because everyone turned on her. She stared at her plate, not seeing the food. She didn't need this. She needed all her energy to revive her career.

Which now depended on Charlie.

She stole another look at him over her glasses and began to really think about Charlie and the new show for the first time. Things weren't nearly as bad as they'd seemed earlier. Charlie had potential. After all, he was intelligent. Verbal. Even occasionally funny. She could make him a star. All she had to do was study him, design a format that fit him and plug him into it. He and his mouth could take it from there, while she goosed the publicity along.

She could have him a household word by Christmas. Three months easy, and she'd be back on top.

She waited until the waitress had brought their dinners, and then she began her pitch. "You're really verbal," she told him, batting her eyelashes at him. "I like that in a man. Especially in a man whose show I'm producing."

Charlie stopped, his fork in midair, and eyed her cautiously. "What's that supposed to mean?"

Allie smiled at him, hearty and encouraging. "I'm going to make you a star, Charlie."

"The hell you are." Charlie went back to his dinner.

Allie pulled back a little and exchanged glances with Joe, who shrugged. Okay, so he'd have to be convinced. No problem. She returned to Charlie and her career. "Look, I know your show was a sort of cult hit in Lawrenceville and you like to do things your way, but you're starting all over here in a bad time slot. And radio is not exactly a secure career, as you well know. I can—"

Charlie pointed his fork at her. "No, you can't. Bill should have told you. I'm temporary. I'm going to be here five or six weeks, tops, probably not that long. I've got places I have to be by November. And this guy whose show I'm covering, Waldo, right?" Allie nodded. "Well, Waldo's coming back."

Allie frowned at him and even Joe blinked.

"Waldo's not coming back," he told Charlie. "He's in San Diego with his sister. Resting comfortably at last report."

Charlie shrugged. "Must be for a visit. Bill knows I'm just temporary."

"Now what's Bill up to?" Joe asked Allie, and she shook her head, clearly as mystified as he was.

Charlie's eyes went from one to the other. "He's not coming back?"

"Waldo shot the console his last night on the air," Allie told him. "He said it was talking to him and wouldn't shut up."

"Maybe he just needs a nice vacation," Charlie suggested.

"Maybe he needs to be away from stereo equipment," Joe said. "He's not coming back."

"So that means," Allie began, ready to make her pitch.

"So that means you're going to be breaking in another guy in about six weeks," Charlie told her. "Do not bother making me a hit. I'm temporary."

He returned to his dinner and began to quiz Joe on Tuttle, and Allie sat back and regrouped. The problem wasn't that he refused to help her make him famous. She could do that without him. She'd made Mark a success without any appreciable input from him.

The problem was that he wasn't going to be around long enough for her to rebuild her career.

Unless she hit the ground running a lot faster than she'd intended.

Allie gave it a minute's thought. All right, she could do that.

And in the meantime, the news made the penicillin

project a lot more possible. If he was only going to be around a few weeks, she could have a one-night fling with him without any consequences. She wasn't used to having flings actually, but she was thirty-six. Her flinging years weren't going to last forever. She had every intention of getting married and having children some day, and then flings would be out of the question. This might be it.

She looked at the situation from all sides. There didn't seem to be any serious obstacles, aside from Charlie himself.

"All right," she said and began to eat her dinner.

Charlie stopped eating and looked at Joe. "Why do I have a bad feeling about her giving in so easily?"

"Because you're a student of human nature," Joe told him.

Allie ignored them both to put her plan into action as soon as they were finished eating. "Let's take Charlie on a tour of the city on our way home. He should see Tuttle a little before he goes on the air tomorrow night. It'll give him something to talk about." *And I can find out what he's interested in and plan a program on it.*

"The tour sounds great." Charlie picked up his check. "But you don't need to put me up. I've got a room at a motel. Thanks for the offer, though."

Not good. She needed to get to know him fast if she was going to get the show moving right away. And then there was the Fling Plan. It was going to be hard enough for her to seduce him in her own apartment. A motel room would be impossible. Allie smiled at him. "I think you should stay with us. You told Mark you were."

Charlie shrugged. "Who cares?"

"Mark won't be mad if you're not staying with us." Allie batted her eyes at him again. It wasn't one of her better skills, but she was desperate.

Charlie leaned close until they were almost nose to nose. "You know, I haven't known you very long, Alice McGuffey, but I can tell you're up to something."

"As I said, a student of human nature." Joe leaned back in his chair to watch.

"Joe will make waffles for breakfast if we ask him nicely." Allie grabbed Charlie's hand again so he couldn't escape. His hand was broad and warm, and she was beginning to feel absolutely cheerful about seducing him. "We can talk about the station tonight. Where's your suitcase? At the motel?"

"Just a duffel bag. It's in my car." Charlie frowned at her. "I still think you're up to something."

Allie tried to look innocent and guileless while she cast around for a selling point. "Joe puts pecans in the waffles."

"I'm probably going to regret this." Charlie looked at Joe. "What do you think?"

Joe shook his head. "I'm staying out of this. Although we do have a couch, and I do put pecans in the waffles." He looked at Allie. "On the other hand, I do think she's up to something."

"They better be great waffles," Charlie said.

"They'll be unforgettable," Allie promised.

CHARLIE WASN'T USED to struggling with his conscience, but then his life wasn't usually this complex. His conscience said, stay away, lie low, don't get involved with these nice people. But he never listened to his conscience, anyway.

He was going to do it, he realized as they got up to go. He was going to move in with Allie and Joe and pump them for background on the station, all the news and rumor that only friends would repeat to friends. It would be low and slimy of him, but it was a great opportunity, and he'd been around long enough to know that great opportunities in life were few and far between.

Just keep your hands off Allie, he told himself sternly. It was one thing to use her for information; it was another thing entirely to use her for.... He glanced down at her, and she smiled, and he remembered how warm she'd been in his arms. Just thinking about her was a bad idea.

Waffles and gossip, yes. Allie, absolutely no.

He excused himself and went to find a phone to cancel his motel reservation. *Remember,* he told himself. *Be virtuous.*

It would be a nice change for him.

"WHAT ARE YOU UP TO?" Joe asked Allie when Charlie had gone.

Allie shoved her chair in, squaring her shoulders. "I'm going to seduce him." It sounded pretty stupid when she said it out loud.

"What?"

"I have a plan. He'll be like penicillin." Joe looked at her as if she were nuts, so she elaborated, warming to her topic as she explained. "Mark's just a bad habit, like a virus. All I need is an antidote. I'll sleep with Charlie, and then I'll be over Mark."

Joe put his head in his hands. "Even for you, this is a dumb idea."

"Why?" Allie blinked down at him. "It's worked great so far. I don't mind about Mark much at all when I'm around Charlie."

"And what are you going to do to get over Charlie?"

"I won't need to get over Charlie. From now on, I'm concentrating on my career. Charlie is just a fling."

Joe looked at her as if she were demented. "Except you're not the kind of woman who has flings. And you're already concentrating too much on your career. That's how you ended up with Mark, because he was *convenient.* And I don't think Charlie is the kind of guy you forget."

"Well, I'm thirty-six," Allie said, exasperated. "If I don't start having flings now, I never will. And I'm tired of getting all wrapped up in a guy and then trying to cope when he's gone. I want a nice, simple, short, purely sexual one-night stand, and then I can forget about Mark. And Charlie's out of here in six weeks, he said so. This is perfect."

Joe spoke very slowly to her. "This. Is. A. Dumb. Idea."

"Listen." Allie fought back the anger that suddenly threatened her voice. "I know how dumb I am. I know Mark is worthless. I knew it when I was with him, but I kept making excuses. And now I'm stuck in this stupid thing where I want to be with him, and I don't even know why. Haven't you ever wanted somebody you knew wasn't worth it?"

"Yes," Joe said. "I imagine almost everybody has."

"Well, all I'm trying to do is get over it." Allie stuck out her chin. "Is that so bad?"

"No." Joe stood up and the sympathy in his eyes almost laid her low. "No, of course not. But Charlie is…well…I don't think I'd mess with Charlie." He looked over her shoulder. "He looks like the kind of guy who makes an impression."

"Not on me." Allie turned and saw Charlie walking toward them. He looked wonderful: big and broad and solid and fun. But not permanent. She could take him or leave him. Or take him *and* leave him. No problem.

Charlie came back to the table and smiled at them. "Let's go. You can tell me all about the station. Leave nothing out, no matter how disgusting. I'm braced for anything."

"Good," Allie said.

THEY GAVE CHARLIE a quick tour of old Tuttle in the late-September dusk. The town unfolded before him like a set of sepia-toned postcards: a white filigree bandstand in the park, a narrow Main Street mercifully free of aluminum storefronts, and a city hall that looked like a glowering, gargoyled sandstone castle.

"Historic preservationists, bless them," Joe told him. "They fight tooth and nail to keep old Tuttle pure. Of course, over on the other side, new Tuttle is a symphony of aluminum siding, but who cares?"

"But even the preservationists can't save city hall," Allie said.

"They're going to tear down that building?" Charlie craned his neck to look back at the ornate structure.

He wasn't a historic-building nut, but tearing down something that magnificently outrageous seemed a waste.

Joe shrugged. "I think they're just going to abandon it. Too hard to heat or something. They've got a new building all planned. There's a model of it in the basement of the old building. It's awful." Joe turned a corner and a few minutes later it was dark.

"What happened?"

"East Tuttle, better known as Eastown." Allie pointed out the window. "See? Streetlights out, but nobody fixes them. This is not a Good Section of Town."

"In defense of the city department, they try." Joe slowed to let a weaving pedestrian cross. "The vandalism around here is pretty frequent."

"Not that frequent," Allie said. "These people get taken for a ride."

Charlie looked around at the peeling paint and broken steps and a derelict corner grocery store, and tried to make it fit with what he'd seen of Tuttle before. "A lot of drugs down here?"

Allie shrugged. "Probably, but I hear the best place to score is right by the old bandstand in the park."

Charlie started to laugh. "So much for Tuttle, the perfect small town."

Allie sighed. "It used to be sort of like that. A lot of mom-and-pop businesses run by people who called you by name. Most of them are gone now, run out by the chains." She peered out the window at another corner store left standing empty. "You know, I don't think there are any independent groceries left in the whole city."

"That's a shame," Charlie said absently. Tuttle was not a hotbed of crime. What the hell could be going on at a radio station in a town like this to make a man like Bill Bonner lose his cool and his father send him in as an amateur detective?

Something here didn't make sense. And since his father and Bill were involved, two men notorious for getting their own way no matter what the cost, Charlie was especially wary. They were up to something.

He sat silently while Joe drove and talked and eventually they came to a slightly better part of town full of old frame houses with big front porches, and Charlie smiled in spite of himself. Tuttle was a nice little town, the kind of town he'd always liked when he'd driven through one on his way to someplace else. He avoided stopping in any town like this one on the grounds that if he really liked it, he'd stay, and then he'd take a permanent job. And if things went the way they usually did, he'd get promoted, and then he'd be in charge, and pretty soon he'd be his father.

No town was worth that.

Then Joe turned again, and in a few minutes they were in a more modern neighborhood, passing a mall.

"Tuttle has a mall?" Charlie asked, amazed.

"There's a lot more to Tuttle than meets the eye," Allie said, and Charlie wondered exactly how much more there was, how much of it Allie knew, and how long it would take him to get it out of her.

IT WAS LATE when they got back to the apartment. They'd picked up Charlie's car at the restaurant and he'd followed them home, parking behind Joe on a side street away from the blare of the traffic. He joined them, and Joe gestured to a three-story white brick house. "This is us. Three apartments. We've got the second floor."

The house was simple but elegant in its proportions, and Charlie felt good just looking at it. "Very nice," he said and followed them up the wide stone steps and into the cream-walled hallway.

It was a great house. A comfortable house.

That made him uneasy. Getting too comfortable would be bad because he was leaving in November. Maybe he'd be better off in a really ugly motel.

"Come on up, Charlie," Allie called to him from the stairway, and her voice was husky, and he began to climb the steps to her without thinking about it.

ALLIE SHOWED HIM around the apartment: a big cream and peach living room with two couches and lots of lamps and bookcases, a white kitchen big enough for a full-size oak table and a mass of cooking gear, a large sea-green bathroom about the size of the bedroom in Charlie's last apartment with an old claw-foot tub about the size of his old bed, and two large bedrooms, one in gray and red for Joe, and one in peach and white for Allie. It confirmed all Charlie's suspicions that Joe and Allie were wonderful, warm, generous people who shouldn't be allowed out without a keeper.

"This is great," Charlie said when they were back in the living room. "But you people are nuts."

Allie flopped down on one of the overstuffed couches. "Why?"

"I'm a complete stranger and you just invited me into your apartment and showed me everything you own." Charlie shook his head at both of them. "You're asking to be ripped off."

"Nope. We know Bill." Joe headed back to the kitchen. "Want something to drink?"

"Iced tea, please," Allie called after him, and Charlie sat down across from her.

"What does Bill have to do with it?"

Allie snuggled down into the couch cushions, and Charlie let his mind wander for a moment. Allie was as well-upholstered as the couch. A comfortable woman. The kind of woman without angles or sharp bones or—

"Bill owns the station," Allie said. "And nothing or nobody gets in the station that Bill doesn't know everything about. If he hired you, he's seen your baby pictures."

Since Bill was Charlie's father's college roommate, this was truer than Allie knew, but Charlie was still not convinced. "You're telling me it's impossible for Bill to have hired a creep? Then how did he get Mark?"

Allie grinned. "You're biased. Mark's not so bad. He's a little insecure, and he's ambitious for his show, but who wouldn't be?"

"Me," Charlie said.

Joe came back in the room bracketing three iced-tea glasses in his hands. "You're not ambitious?" he asked as Charlie took one.

"Nope. I'm just here to have a good time." Charlie leaned back and sipped his tea. It was full and rich, sun tea laced with just enough lemon and sugar. He settled more comfortably into the couch. "And it's a good thing I'm not ambitious since I'm on from 10:00 to 2:00 a.m.''

Allie smiled at him brightly. It was a smile he was learning to associate with Positive Career Talk. ''The time could be a lot better,'' she told him. ''But don't worry. I'm going to make you a star.''

''No, you are not.'' Charlie narrowed his eyes at her. The only thing that was going to save him was that he was on late enough that nobody would notice how inept he was. All he needed was Allie drawing attention to him as he stuck a microphone in his eye or something, and then questions would be asked. ''Don't you even think about holding up a cue card for me. I told you. I don't want to be a star.''

Joe snorted. ''You don't have any choice. If Allie wants you famous, you're going to be famous.''

''Forget it,'' Charlie told Allie. ''Wipe the thought from your mind.''

''We can talk about it later,'' Allie said smoothly. ''Now, tomorrow night's your first show and I thought—''

''Don't.'' Charlie scowled at her. ''Thinking is bad for a woman. Tell me about the other people at the station. I already know about Mark and Lisa.''

Allie sat silent with her tea, obviously regrouping, so Joe chimed in. ''Bill owns the station and theoretically runs it as general manager.''

''Theoretically?''

Joe exchanged a glance with Allie. ''His wife, Beattie, decided about six months ago that she wanted a career. Bill gives Beattie anything she wants, so she's pretty much running the place now.''

Charlie quirked an eyebrow at Joe. This was news Bill hadn't shared. "Is that good?"

"I think so," Joe said. "She fired Weird Waldo."

"He thought Martians were invading the station through the consoles," Allie said. "He kept announcing during his show that they were getting closer. It was actually kind of interesting if you suspended logical thought. Beattie wanted him gone, but Bill said he was just being colorful."

"And then he shot the console," Charlie said.

"Yep, just last week. Blew the whole thing away." Allie sighed. "At least we gained a new console. And lost Waldo, thanks to Beattie."

"Wouldn't even Bill have fired him at that point?" Charlie asked, incredulous.

"Bill's ability to ignore anything unpleasant is legendary," Joe told him.

"Great." Charlie drank more of his iced tea. If Bill could ignore somebody shooting up a broadcasting booth, the one anonymous letter that had made him call for help must have been a beauty. He brought his attention back to Joe. "What else should I know?"

They talked on into the night, Joe and Allie filling him in on the rest of the station personnel, like Albert the anal-retentive business manager who recited ad prices in his sleep, and Marcia the ambitious afternoon DJ who was breathing down Mark's neck for the prime-time slot, and Karen the receptionist who knew all the gossip not fit to print, and Harry the Howler who was on right before Charlie.

"Harry howls from six to ten," Allie told Charlie. "He likes to think he's wild and crazy, but he's really sweet with the volume turned up. His real area of expertise is cars, so if you ever have problems with yours, ask Harry.''

"And then there's me.''

Allie nodded. "Yep. Harry's audience usually starts to fade about nine, nine-thirty, and then we had Weird Waldo."

Charlie tried not to show his relief. "So, at the moment, my show has a listening audience of about…''

Allie grinned at him. "Oh, six or seven, tops. And they're all listening because they're concerned about the Martians, and they're waiting for the update.''

Charlie started to laugh. "Oh, God. This is going to be awful.''

"Then at two o'clock, there's Grady.''

"Tell me Grady's normal.''

"Well…'' Allie stopped, obviously searching for the words to describe Grady. "Grady is sweet. He talks about things like the life force and crystal power and personal auras, and then he plays classical guitar music and Gregorian chants and other…'' She stopped. "I can't describe Grady. His show is very soothing, and he has his own small but fanatically loyal following.'' She shrugged. "I like him. Grady's a good person.''

"If he has only a small following, why is he still on the air?''

"Because he's Grady Bonner. Someday, all this will be his.''

"The son and heir? Then why is he on the grave-yard shift?''

"Because his following is small. Bill gave Grady two to six to keep him off the streets.''

Charlie took a deep breath. "So I'm sandwiched in

between Howling Harry and Grady 'I Have Lived In Other Times' Bonner?''

''That's about it.''

It couldn't be better. No one would ever hear him. He started to grin. ''I'm in big trouble.''

''No, you're not.'' Allie leaned forward. ''From ten to two, you have a lot of freedom. This is so all the really knee-jerk conservatives go to bed early so they can get up with the chickens, which means your audience, once you build one, will be open to new things. As long as you don't do anything that upsets Bill, you can say anything you want. We can do this, Charlie. We—''

''No, we can't.'' Charlie hated to ruin her plans, she looked so cute trying to sell them to him, but he was not going to be a success. ''I don't want to be famous. I just want a nice little radio show for a few weeks. That's all.''

Allie shoved her glasses back up her nose. ''But, Char-lie—''

''No,'' Charlie said firmly.

Joe stood up. ''I'd love to stay and watch this, but I have to go to work in the morning. Good night, all.''

He disappeared into the bathroom, and Charlie leaned back on the couch.

''I think we should talk about this,'' Allie said.

''I don't,'' Charlie said, but Allie did anyway, explaining all the good things that would come his way if he just put himself in her hands.

She was a good persuader, and under any other circumstances he might have listened just because she talked such a good fight, but he was only temporary. He wasn't staying. He wasn't going to be a success.

He wouldn't mind being in her hands, though.

He jerked his mind away from the thought when Joe came out of the bathroom in his robe.

"Bathroom's all yours. Good night." Joe looked at Allie and shook his head, and then he went into his bedroom and closed the door.

Charlie frowned at Allie. She'd abandoned her argument about his career and was now looking at him as if she was sizing him up. He had the damnedest feeling she was going to try a new attack. It wasn't a reassuring feeling. "Why did Joe shake his head?"

"What?" Allie stood up and moved to stand beside him, smiling brightly. "Never mind. My bedroom, as you know, is on the left. Want to see it again?"

"Come here, McGuffey." He pulled her down beside him, trapping her hand in his. "What are you up to? Tell me everything, now. I can take it."

"I was going to tell you, anyway." She sat stiff and straight. "I just wanted to be in my nightgown to do it."

"Your nightgown." Charlie clamped down on his evil thoughts and patted her hand. "Well, I'm sorry I'm going to miss that. Why your nightgown?"

She sighed. "Joe thinks this is a bad idea."

"Joe's no dummy. If he thinks it is, it probably is."

"I think so, too. Forget it." She stood up, and he caught her hand.

"Oh, no, you don't. Just in case you change your mind, I need to be prepared. Are we going to go Vaseline Mark's car windows? Put Tabasco in Lisa's diaphragm?"

Allie sat down again next to him. "All right. I have a favor to ask."

Charlie tried to look encouraging. "Shoot." Allie looked so uncomfortable, he was ready for anything.

She took a deep breath. "I want you to sleep with me."

CHARLIE DIDN'T SAY anything, and she stole a glance at him.

He looked stunned.

She should have know it wouldn't work. She wasn't the seductress type. She flopped back against the couch, defeated. "I know it's dumb, but I had this plan. I thought maybe if I slept with somebody else, I'd get over Mark permanently. Sort of like getting right back on the horse after you've been thrown."

Charlie made a sound like a strangled laugh.

"What did you say?"

"I whinnied."

Allie fought back a smile. "You laughed. Okay, go ahead. I just…" The words were too dumb to say out loud, so she shut up and shrugged instead.

Charlie leaned back beside her. "Why don't you tell me about it?"

Allie hesitated and then gave in. "Well, it's hard to explain without sounding stupid. Everybody at the station thinks Mark is God. We were working together, making the show a hit, and when we started dating, it just felt right, I guess." She wrinkled her nose as she thought. "And he was really good to me." She turned her head to look Charlie in the eye, trying to make him understand. "I know he wasn't impressive today, but he really was good to me. I've never been that anxious to settle down, but I thought we'd be together forever, working on the show." She shook her head in disgust. "I was stupid. But it was still hard to give up. And I still miss it." She stopped and frowned. "But you know, I think I miss the relationship more than I miss him."

Charlie shook his head. "Everybody at the station thinks he's God? They must be morons."

"Not all of them. Just me."

Charlie frowned at her. "If you're going to feel sorry for yourself, get off my couch and go to your room."

Allie relaxed back into the couch. "You know, I'm a very good producer. I just can't handle my personal life."

Charlie snorted. "You and about twenty million other people."

She rolled her head sideways to look at him. "How do you do it?"

Charlie grinned at her. "Not very well. I have this commitment problem."

"You and about twenty million other guys." Allie grinned back. "Big deal. I bet once it's over for you, it's over. I bet you don't go on obsessing about it afterward."

"No. But then I've never loved anyone enough to obsess about it."

"Well, that's just my point." She sat up again. "I'm not sure I loved Mark. I didn't even *like* Mark much toward the end, which may be one of the reasons he dumped me. But I was used to being with him, working on the show, you know? I'm just…stuck in this stupid rut, and I need something to bounce me out of it."

Charlie looked confused but not condemning. "So,

your plan was that we'd sleep together, and then what?''

"Then I'd be over Mark, and we'd go to work."

"A short-term arrangement." He sounded noncommittal, which wasn't encouraging.

Allie tried to get back to selling the idea. "Absolutely. A one-night stand. No strings. The last thing in the world I need right now is another relationship." The thought of trying to keep another man happy made her tired all by itself. "I'm just sick of feeling like I'm going to throw up every time I see Mark."

"You and about twenty million other people."

Allie laughed. "No, really." She tried to be serious. "He's a nice guy. Lots of people like him. His show is very popular. And he takes a nice publicity picture."

"Oh, that's important in radio."

Allie turned to look at him when she heard the scorn in his voice. "Oh? And what do you do in radio?"

Charlie tensed for a moment and then relaxed deeper into the couch. "Well, there used to be a really late show in Lawrenceville from two to six. After Two with Ten Tenniel." He grinned down at her and she grinned back because it was impossible not to. "Strange people call from two to six. I'm hoping the ten-to-two people are at least half as bizarre."

His voice was low but it kept his grin in it when he talked. That was one of things she liked best about him, although actually, there was a lot to like about Charlie. She leaned a little closer to him. "You like bizarre? Then you're going to love WBBB."

"I love bizarre. That's why I let you pick me up." He looked down at her, and she could have sworn she saw heat in his eyes. But then, what did she know about men?

Charlie stood up and pulled her off the couch. "Go to bed, Allie, so I can go to bed. You get the bathroom first." He patted her shoulder. "I'll help you with Mark tomorrow, *not* by sleeping with you, but now I've got to get some real sleep."

Well, that was that. Allie walked back to her bedroom door. She should have known it wouldn't work.

Rats.

Unless…

CHARLIE WATCHED her walk toward her bedroom and tried to feel virtuous for turning her down. He did feel virtuous. He'd made a great sacrifice. There was nothing he wanted more than to be in Allie's hands.

In Allie's bed.

Oh, hell.

Feeling virtuous was a lousy trade for what he was giving up.

Allie stopped, and then turned back to him, a much too innocent look on her face. "How about a smaller favor?"

"Smaller than sex?"

"Yes." She drifted back to him, and he felt wary again.

"What?"

Allie took off her glasses and lifted her chin. "Kiss me. So I can concentrate this time. I missed it the last time. In the bar."

Charlie ran his fingers through his hair. All his instincts told him to run, but she was standing there with that great mouth, and he wanted it. "You really are something. You treat all the guys you meet like this?"

Allie shook her head, and he watched the light glint in her hair as it swung back and forth. "Nope. You just happened to hit me on a very unusual day."

"Lucky me." Charlie swallowed and surrendered. "Okay, pucker up, but this time, pay attention. I don't want to have to keep on doing this."

She nodded. "Right."

Allie lifted her face to his, and he bent and kissed her. He meant to make it brief, but the softness of her mouth moved against his and took his breath away. *I'm in big trouble here,* he thought, and then he stopped thinking.

He felt her hand on his cheek, and he closed his eyes. She was intoxicating, and he opened his mouth and teased her lips with his tongue until she opened to him and he could taste her. Her body moved against him, and he held her close, moving his hands up to her shoulders and then back down to the small of her back, pressing her hips close to his, soft against him.

When he finally broke the kiss, they were both breathless.

"Thank you," Allie said unsteadily as she stepped back. "That was very nice. Good night." She backed away into the bathroom and shut the door.

Charlie sat down on the couch and tried to remember where he was.

He was not going to get involved with Allie. He had a job to worry about. He was going to lay low. He was going to not make waves. He was going to do his job and get out. He was going to forget Allie and get some sleep.

He unbuttoned his shirt and went to find his bag. He didn't have pajamas, but with Allie flitting about making suggestions, he had to wear something. He found his sweatpants just as Allie came out of the bathroom in a long blue cotton nightgown. She looked very virginal.

"Here are your sheets and things," she said, putting them on the end of the couch. "Do you need anything else?"

Charlie clamped down on his wayward thoughts. "No. Thank you."

"Good night." She hesitated, and then she went into her room.

He took his sweatpants and his toothbrush into the bathroom. *Don't think about her,* he told himself. He got ready for bed, concentrating on not thinking about Allie, and then he went out to the couch and made his bed, concentrating on not thinking about Allie, and then he got into his bed, concentrating on not thinking about Allie.

It wasn't working.

ALLIE LAY in bed and thought about Charlie.

God, he was beautiful, standing there in the living room with his shirt unbuttoned. She'd never been turned on just looking at a man before, but he was so broad and beautiful. And dangerous.

If they were on TV instead of radio, she'd make him leave his shirt unbuttoned. Women would be clawing at the set.

And then there was his mouth. Kissing like that should be illegal. Or at least licensed.

She put her hands over her face and groaned. Sleep-

ing with Charlie would not be penicillin. Sleeping with
Charlie would be cocaine. Of all the stupid ideas she'd
had in her life, this was the stupidest.

Why didn't she ever listen to Joe?

She turned over onto her side, concentrating on not
thinking about Charlie.

God, he looked good. And he kissed better.

She buried her head under the pillow and tried to
think about her career.

CHARLIE ROLLED OVER on the couch. Sleeping with
Allie would be wrong. She was emotionally vulnerable
right now. By tomorrow, she'd be relieved he hadn't
taken her up on her offer.

Of course, by tomorrow, he'd be insane with frustration.

It was that damn kiss. If she hadn't asked for the
kiss, he wouldn't be thinking about how soft her
mouth was, how soft she was all over...

He rolled over again, trying to think about the anonymous letter and how he didn't have a clue about what
a disc jockey did and how tomorrow night he'd have
to do it, concentrating on everything and anything but
Allie.

She was probably asleep by now, anyway.

It was thinking about her mouth that was the worst.

ALLIE SAT UP in bed and put her arms around her
knees.

Not thinking about Charlie wasn't working. She was
breathless with not thinking about him. She wanted
him. She physically itched for him. This wasn't the
gauzy need she'd always assumed women felt for the

men they lusted after. This was unpleasant and uncomfortable and would require full body contact to satiate.

And he'd already said no once.

Suppose she just strolled out there.

And then what? Took off her nightgown? Did the dance of the seven veils? That would never work. She was a lousy dancer. Production was her specialty, not seduction. Maybe if she made up some cue cards: "Yes, Allie, I'd love to sleep with you. Take off your clothes."

Right, that would work.

Besides, he was probably already asleep.

She put her head on her knees and moaned softly. She was never going to get to sleep.

CHARLIE SAT UP and put his head in his hands. He was never going to get to sleep. He wanted her so much now, he throbbed with it. How the hell had this happened?

What difference did it make?

He threw off the covers and stood up.

He'd just knock on her door. She was probably asleep. Then he'd go back to the couch and go to sleep.

Right.

He picked up his shaving kit and pulled out a strip of condoms, shoving them in the pocket of his sweats before he went to her door.

He knocked softly. "Allie?"

"Come in," she said.

She was sitting up in bed, her arms wrapped around her knees and her glossy brown hair tangled around her face. "I can't sleep," she said.

"Me, neither." He sat down beside her. "You and your one last kisses." He cradled her cheek in his hand. "Do you still want that one-night stand?"

"Yes," she breathed, and the heat flared in him.

"Thank God." He slid his arm around her. "Move over."

Three

Charlie moved pretty fast for a big guy, shoving off his sweatpants and sliding her nightgown over her head while she drew a sharp breath at his touch. The heat flared in her when the shock of his skin touched hers, and he touched her everywhere. She clutched him to her, tipping her head back for his mouth as if the muscles in her neck had given way. His hands moved over her, stroking her back, her sides, sliding down to pull her close to the hardness of his hips, and all the while he tormented her mouth with his tongue. He was everywhere, and wherever he was, there was heat.

"Tell me what you want," he whispered against her mouth, and she clung to him and whispered back, "You."

He moved down her throat to the hollow between her neck and shoulder, making her squirm as he found the nerve there. He trailed more hot kisses down her shoulder until his mouth found her breast and she forgot who she was. He dallied there, sucking hard until she could feel the pull and tingle deep inside her. She moved against him convulsively, pressing him to her, and he moved his mouth to her other breast and made her moan again.

Allie drowned in the heat; waves of it washed over her as Charlie moved against her. Then his mouth found hers again and he was kissing her hard, his tongue thrusting into her mouth as he pulled her on top of him and pressed her head to his so that she couldn't escape his kiss. She stretched against him, drunk with desire, and he rolled over so she was under him again and moved his hand between them, lower this time.

His whisper tickled her ear and made her squirm. "You have a beautiful body, Allie. You were made for love." He slid his hand between her legs and she gasped and arched up to meet him.

"Don't ever stop touching me," she said thickly. Her skin prickled, and the pounding came stronger, in rhythm with his hand. "Don't ever, ever stop."

But he did, rolling away from her to reach for something on the floor. She heard foil tearing.

"Charlie?"

She struggled to sit up and then his mouth was on hers again, his hands on her hips, his body against hers. He pulled her under him and then he was sliding into her, and she felt her entire body clench and throb as he rocked into her, felt herself drawn into the pounding in her blood, in his blood, the pounding everywhere.

"Wait." She felt herself lurch out of control. "Wait. I can't…"

"Let go," he whispered in her ear. "Let go, Allie."

She clutched at him, and he stared down at her hotly, half in shadow, his eyes glittering as he thrust into her over and over again. *Who is he?* she thought. *I don't even* know *him. And he's inside me.*

Then he moaned and his head dropped to her shoulder, and she felt his grasp tighten on her as he slumped over her. She held him to her, rocking him a little, feeling warm and tingly and shaken and relieved and disappointed.

Charlie rolled off and pulled her close to him.

"I lost you along the way," he said, still breathless. "What did I do wrong?"

"Nothing." Allie settled against him, trying not to be annoyed. "That was incredible. You were wonderful." For a moment, it was like being with Mark again, and she sighed in resignation. Men were obviously not her strong suit.

Charlie held her until his breathing slowed, and then he propped himself up on one elbow and looked down at her, moving his hand up to cup her breast again. "You were with me there," he whispered. "I could feel it in you."

"I don't know." She tried to smile her usual supportive-lover smile at him, but she was distracted by his stroking thumb. "It doesn't matter."

He bent and kissed her cheek softly. "What part threw you off?" He moved his mouth to her breast. "Was it this?" He ran his tongue over her, and her body tightened at his touch.

"No." She moved against his mouth, her annoyance fading considerably. "No. It wasn't anything you did."

His hand moved down and stroked her gently. "This?"

"No," she breathed, and closed her eyes to concentrate on his touch.

"Allie?" He kissed her until she clung to him, dizzy again.

"I love it when you touch me." She moved under his hand as he stroked her.

"Good. I'll do it often." His fingers were stroking faster, and she found it hard to concentrate on his words. The pressure was everywhere, growing stronger, and she moved against the hard barrier of his body when she felt the itch start under her skin again.

"I won't let anything happen to you," he whispered, one arm tight around her. "Let go. I'm holding you."

Allie clung to him, drunk with the pressure, aching for release. The whole world was his hand against her, and the prickle in her blood, and she buried her face against his chest as she felt the pressure wind tighter, and she knew she was was going to explode if he didn't stop. Out of control.

"Oh, God." Allie tried to move away, but Charlie rolled and pinned her under him, thrusting his tongue in her ear, and she twisted at the shocking pleasure of it, crying out once as the pressure flared in her and her skin screamed, and then everything did explode, the heat arcing through her body as she gasped in his arms.

Charlie held her so tightly she had trouble breathing, but she clutched him to her anyway.

"Allie? Allie, love?"

She buried her face against his chest and tried to stop gasping, but the waves still lapped gently inside her, like little aftershocks.

"Allie?"

She clung to him, trying to find her voice, any coherent thought. "Oh, God, Charlie."

He held her tighter. "I thought you'd gone mute on me."

Allie took a long shuddering breath and then another until sanity returned. The heat and the release settled into her bones like a narcotic. She stretched against him, all her muscles aching, her skin sliding warm against his. "Oh." She drew another deep breath. "I may never talk again."

Charlie brushed her hair back from her face. "Can you sleep now?"

"Only if you don't touch me," she said, and he laughed and pulled her close, and she curled into him, and then they both fell asleep.

ALLIE WOKE UP when the sunlight flooded the room. She'd rolled away from Charlie in the night, but his hand was still on her waist, and she liked the weight and heat of it there. She lay very still and savored how good her body still felt, and only gradually did she become aware of Joe in the kitchen, banging pans.

As flings went, this one had been a beauty. No guilt, no fear, no emotion at all, really, except pleasure. Bless Charlie. And now she was going to make him a star. Life had done a one-hundred-and-eighty-degree turn on her overnight. She couldn't wait to get started again.

She stirred a little and felt Charlie's hand tighten on her waist in his sleep, and she moved her head on the pillow to look at him. His blond-brown hair was tousled and his eyelashes were like smudges on his cheeks, and he looked like a fallen angel.

It really was too bad they weren't doing TV.

She eased a little closer, and his arm gathered her to him until his cheek brushed against her hair.

"Morning," he said without opening his eyes. "How do you feel?"

Allie grinned against his chest. "Very smug, now that I know what all the shouting was about."

Charlie laughed softly. "You should know. You were the one doing the shouting."

Allie jerked her head back. "What?"

He smiled at her and kissed her forehead. "You scream when you come."

"I do not."

"The hell you don't." He gathered her back to him and sighed happily. "But it takes a lot of the guesswork out of making love to you, so I'm not complaining."

Allie thought about pushing him away and decided against it. "Very funny."

There was another crash from the kitchen.

Allie smiled again. "Joe's making breakfast. Aren't you hungry?"

"Yes." He kissed the top of her head. "But I've got to check out Tuttle in the daylight. So I'll just take a rain check, if that's okay with you."

"And miss Joe's waffles?"

"Hell, no. I'm eating waffles." Charlie rolled up on one arm and looked down at her. "I'm taking a rain check on you. Until tonight." He slid his hand under the sheet and cupped her breast, caressing her. "Same time, same place, same screams?"

He was gorgeous in the sunlight, and he had golden hands. She felt dizzy under them right now. But he was also her career. Mixing sex and business would be bad. Look what had happened with Mark.

"I thought we were a one-night stand." Her hand closed over his to stop his caress, but somehow she ended up pressing his hand against her, instead.

"We are." Charlie climbed over her to get out of bed, pulling the sheet down to kiss her breast on his way. "One night at a time."

She pulled the sheet back up and squinted myopically to watch him put on his sweatpants, admiring the muscles in his legs and his rear while she told herself she should stop now, that sleeping with Charlie was not a good idea, that he was leaving in November. Her brain told her to tell him she didn't want another night.

Her mouth flatly refused to say anything that stupid.

Something in her face must have tipped him off to her quandary because he stopped tying the string on his pants and grew serious. "You can always say no," he told her.

To you? The thought was so ludicrous, she laughed. "I'll try to remember that," she told him, and her spirits rose again. Enough of this chitchat. She had a career to resuscitate, and Charlie was a one-man rescue squad. She threw off the top quilt and got out of bed, fighting to keep the sheet wrapped around her, but it slipped as she yanked it free from the mattress.

Charlie approved. "The hell with the waffles." He reached for her, but she danced out of the way, blushing and covering herself with her hand and the corner of the sheet.

"Go eat." She flapped her free hand at him. "You need fuel for that body. You must be running on empty now."

"We get off at 2:00 a.m." He grinned while she grabbed her robe and tried to put it on without dropping the sheet. "We can be home by two-thirty. You don't want my side of the bed empty, do you?"

She tied her robe closed and stuck her chin out, taking control. "You don't have a side, and I'll be asleep by two thirty-five."

"Then you'll be awake by two thirty-six." Charlie grabbed the belt on her robe as she sidled past and caught her to him. He kissed her thoroughly, and then, while she was still reeling, he let her go and walked out of the room, whistling.

Hurry up, two thirty-six, she thought, and then she sat down on the edge of the bed again to get her thoughts back to her career, where they belonged.

"PECANS, right?" Charlie said to Joe who was pouring batter onto the griddle.

"Pecans." Joe closed the iron and turned to Charlie, his arms folded. "So, how did you sleep?"

Charlie sat down and tried to look innocent. "Am I going to get a lecture? Because she made the first move, I swear."

Joe rolled his eyes. "I know. She had a plan."

"Getting over Mark." Charlie nodded and poured some orange juice. "What a loser that guy is."

Joe leaned against the stove. "She has a tendency to pick losers. She has what might be described as a real genius for it."

Charlie winced. "Don't beat around the bush. Say what you mean."

"The only thing that's saved her is that her exes

were lousy lovers. When they went, she wasn't missing much."

"I kind of got that impression last night."

"That's not all you got." Joe opened the iron and pried the waffles out onto a plate. "You don't exactly make love quietly." He put the plate in front of Charlie.

"That's Allie." Charlie was lavish with the syrup. "She's a screamer. Surprised the hell out of me."

"Allie's not the only one. You've got a nice deep moan yourself."

"Me?" Charlie stopped, surprised.

"The walls are thin here," Joe said charitably.

"I'm sorry we kept you up." Charlie took a bite of waffle. "You make a mean waffle. Do I get seconds?"

"Of the waffles, yes. Of Allie…" Joe shrugged. "That's my question. Was last night just an extremely vocal one-night stand or will you be back?"

Charlie stopped chewing. "Well, I was planning on coming back. We can go to a motel if we bother you. That's only fair."

"The noise isn't what bothers me." Joe sat down and started on his own waffles. "What I'm worried about is Allie. Are you going to hurt her? Because if you are, I'm against it."

Charlie stopped chewing, shocked. "I don't hurt people."

"What if Allie's in love with you?"

"She's not."

"She will be if you hang around." Joe pointed at him with a waffle-filled fork. "You're smart, you're funny, and you obviously know how to make her happy in bed."

Charlie thought about the job he'd come to do, and about how fast he'd be out of town when it was done. He sighed. "You're right. I have no serious intentions about Allie. I just like sleeping with her. So I'll do a fade." The thought was extremely unattractive, so he changed the subject. "You know, it's a shame you're gay. You're probably the perfect guy for her."

Joe grinned at him. "It's a shame you're not. You could be the perfect guy for me."

Charlie shook his head. "Probably not. I'm not the perfect guy for anybody."

"Good morning, all." Allie drifted into the kitchen and poured herself a glass of orange juice, smiling a lovely serene smile at both of them. All her tightness was gone. She looked confident and sexy, and they stared at the transformation.

Her smile faded as they stared. "Can I have waffles, too?" she asked Joe finally, and he blinked and then got up to make them for her.

"I've got to find my shoes and then we can make plans," she told Charlie. She smiled at him again, igniting him, and then she drifted back to her bedroom.

Charlie was halfway out of his chair to follow her before he realized it. "Oh, hell." He turned and looked at Joe. "You were right. I should have stayed on that damn couch."

"Maybe you'd better forget about doing the fade." Joe turned back to the waffle iron. "This could be a good thing. She looks invincible."

"She looks like…" Charlie stopped.

"She looks like she's had great sex," Joe said. "It's a new look for her. I'd pay money to see Mark's face when he sees her."

"Yeah? Well, what happens to that look when I stop sleeping with her?"

"Hey, I also saw the look on your face. What makes you think you can stop?"

Charlie put his fork down. Allie was absolutely not part of his plan. His plan was to do the job and get out.

And now there was Allie.

The look he gave Joe was pathetic.

Joe laughed.

WHEN SHE CAME BACK, Allie was wearing her day clothes: a plain, long, brown jersey dress and a man's brown and cream tweed jacket. She looked extremely round and soft, and Charlie reminded himself sternly that from now on, they had a working relationship only.

Then he watched her lick syrup off her fork and for the first time in his life, he envied silverware.

"We don't have to be at the station until four," she told him around bites of waffle.

"That's fine," Charlie replied. He needed some time alone to get his act together. "I want to wander around Tuttle on my own for a while. Get the feel of the place."

"Okay." Allie nodded at him. "I'll meet you in front of the station."

Joe left for an appointment, and Charlie and Allie talked about Tuttle and waffles and washed the dishes, and Charlie fought the feeling he was slipping into, that he'd always known her, that he always would. She was having a weird effect on him: she felt comfortable. Every internal alarm he had was screaming, but she smiled at him and he didn't care.

Out on the street, Allie twirled around on the sidewalk and her dress swirled out around her and she looked so happy, and she had such great legs, that Charlie abandoned all his qualms for the moment and just enjoyed the sunlight and Allie. If he wanted something to worry about, he didn't need to start with Allie; he had the anonymous letter and his first-ever radio show that night.

"Don't forget to meet me at four so I can introduce you to everybody before they leave at five," Allie said, and he promised and then escaped.

Stay away from that woman as much as you can, he warned himself.

Then he thought about meeting her at four and grinned.

WBBB WAS ON THE fourth floor of a bank—"Bill's bank," Allie told him—and Charlie watched her smack open the double glass doors of the station as if she were attacking the place.

Instead of running for cover, the people inside converged on her like a last hope.

The dark-haired receptionist was the first to shriek at her as Allie blew past her with a "Hey, Karen."

"Wait, Allie, I need to talk to you," Karen said, but then the rest of the people began to come out of the narrow hall in front of them, one by one, like clowns out of a toy car.

Lisa darted out first. "Allie, can I have a minute? I need—"

"Allie!" A towheaded man the size of a small

mountain lumbered toward her and slung his arm around her shoulder. "I need to talk to you. Alone."

A much smaller man in a too-tight tie with a too-tight face pushed between them. "Not now, Harry. Alice, the ratings—"

A steely-eyed brunette appeared behind him and shouldered him aside. "Forget it, Albert. I just heard about this mess. I don't give a damn if Mark is dumb enough to dump you, *I'm* not."

Charlie watched Lisa wince, and then saw Allie pat her arm. "One at a time," Allie said, and Harry said, "Wait a minute," and Karen said, "Please, Allie," and Lisa said, "Oh, Allie, I need your help," and Albert said, "The *ratings,* Allie," and then from the hall someone said, "That's enough," and the whole room froze.

Charlie looked beyond the clump of people to the small, slender, older woman standing in the hallway.

"Nothing is changing," she said. "Alice is not leaving her position as Mark's producer."

"Well, actually, Beattie, I am." Allie reached out through the throng that surrounded her and grabbed Charlie by the bicep to drag him to her side. "This is Charlie Tenniel, our new DJ. I have some very exciting ideas for his program."

Charlie opened his mouth to object, but then Beattie spoke and it seemed like a bad idea to interrupt her.

"Bill did not discuss this with me first." The look in Beattie's eye said that Bill had paid dearly for this. "I was most disappointed in him."

"Well, I was, too," Allie said, and Charlie raised an eyebrow at her, surprised at her candor. Then his eyes went back to Beattie. Neat iron-gray hair, trim iron-gray suit, sharp iron-gray eyes. Not the kind of woman you lied to, Beattie. "But now I've met Charlie," Allie went on. "I think this is going to be interesting."

Beattie turned those gray eyes on Charlie, and he tried not to swallow. She surveyed him, starting at the top of his head and moving slowly to his feet before she started back up again. She made the return trip with a gleam in her eye.

Then she turned to Allie. "Oh. I see. Very well." She held out her hand to Charlie. "Very nice to meet you again, Charles. The last time we met, you were five, so I doubt you remember. How are your father and mother?"

Well, Mother is still insisting that Ten was framed when some undesirable planted all that coke on him, and Dad has lost his mind to the point of sending me here, but otherwise they're still golfing and drinking rum punch. "Just fine, Mrs. Bonner, thank you for asking."

Beattie's eyes narrowed for an instant, and Charlie reminded himself not to take Beattie Bonner for granted. She might be pushing seventy, but she was probably sharper than anyone else in the room, himself included.

Sharper than anyone, with the possible exception of Allie. When Charlie turned back to her, she was dispatching people with a warm efficiency that got them off her back without leaving them exasperated. She promised Marcia all the help she needed, Lisa a meeting as soon as she'd shown Charlie around, Harry a conference later that night before his show, Albert an analysis of the ratings by morning, and Karen the first minute she could spare. By the time she was finished, they were alone in the lobby except for Karen looking woebegone behind her desk, and Charlie had a new appreciation of how he'd ended up in Allie's bed the night before.

He also had a new apprehension for his immediate future. "Listen," he told her sternly. "I don't want to be famous."

"Of course not." She smiled up at him. "Let me show you the station."

Charlie followed her with foreboding, but the station itself was innocuous. Aside from the offices, the place was small, white, clean and uncluttered. One dedicated broadcast booth with a production room outside it, one combination broadcast and production room, one tape library, one room with the satellite feed, one conference/break room, and finally Allie's office.

Allie opened the door at the end of the hall of offices and gestured him in. "Welcome to my world."

"This is nice," Charlie said doubtfully as he looked around the tiny cubicle. Every square inch of three of the walls was covered with photos, handwritten notes, magazine articles, old scripts and anything else that Allie felt was valuable and that could be push-pinned up. It was like being inside a very messy desk drawer. The last wall was bookcases filled with reference books and loose-leaf binders and various treasures that Allie had stuffed there for some reason: a soapstone seal, a large rock, a ceramic goblet, a china doll, a bowl of shells. The center of the little room was crowded with an old teacher's desk, two thrift-store carved walnut chairs and a white filing cabinet with a stuffed owl on it. Charlie stared fascinated into the owl's eyes while Allie sat down behind her desk and began to search through the piles of papers.

If they ever made love in this office, he was going to throw his shirt over that owl so it wouldn't watch them. Not that there was room to lie down in here. They'd have to use the desk. Or against the wall... Charlie shook his head to clear it of the thought. He was definitely not going to be pressing Allie up against that wall—

"Your first appointment is with me to talk about how you're going to structure your four hours. Ah ha!" She held up her coffee cup, triumphant. "Also, you might want to start thinking about explaining your program ideas when we meet with Bill at five."

Charlie frowned at her, glad to bring his mind back to the problem at hand. "What's to explain?"

"He likes to preapprove the ideas." Allie looked dubiously into her cup and turned it upside down to shake it. Nothing fell out.

"He approves everything that goes out from this place?"

"Well, not Mark's stuff. Bill loves Mark." Allie got up and took a loose-leaf binder from her bookshelf. "Here's the WBBB handbook—Bill's personal philosophy of broadcasting. You're going to hate it."

Charlie took the book, opened it, read a page and sighed. Bill made Jesse Helms look liberal. "So Bill really does run the station? I thought maybe he'd be one of those distant owners who just drops by to read the profit sheet."

"He used to be."

Charlie looked up at the tone in Allie's voice. "But?"

Allie leaned back in her chair. "But then about six months ago, Beattie decided she wanted a job, so he gave her the run of the place. That upset the station manager and he quit. So Beattie took that job and now she really runs the station."

Charlie raised his eyebrows. "But you said last night she's not bad at it."

Allie nodded. "She's a fast learner, and she's not stupid in the slightest."

"And Bill just gave her the station." Charlie sat back. "Which parts aren't you mentioning?"

Allie bit her lip for a moment. Then she pushed her glasses up her nose and leaned forward. "Beattie doesn't particularly want to talk about this, so don't mention it. Last January, she was diagnosed with breast cancer. She had surgery and her doctor recommended some intensive chemo, and she was in pretty bad shape for a while. Then she started to get better, and in April, when she said she wanted to learn about radio…" Allie shrugged. "If Bill hadn't already owned a station, he'd have bought one for her."

"Well, it must beat chemo."

"She was done in July. And she's doing really well now, and good things have come of it."

"Such as?" Charlie prompted.

"Well, Grady has never been Bill's favorite son, but he stuck with his mom through the whole thing, taking her to chemo, cooking for her when she wouldn't eat, that kind of stuff. Bill hasn't called Grady a moron for months."

Charlie grinned. "I can see where that would be a step up."

"And Beattie's running the station just fine."

Charlie nodded as the pieces fell into place. Beattie had come in cold off the street and the station was still doing fine. Beattie had had some help. "It's doing fine because you showed her the ropes."

Allie shrugged. "I helped a little."

Charlie thought back to the scene in the hall. "Right. Why didn't you ask for the station manager's job?"

Allie looked horrified. "Business? Please, I'd rather die."

Well, he could sympathize with that. "Beattie would give you Mark's show back."

"I don't want Mark's show." Allie met his eyes. "I want Mark's time slot. The drive-time slot. That's where we're going to end up, Charlie."

"At 6:00 a.m.?" Charlie's voice broke in outrage. "In the morning a.m.? Are you nuts, woman?"

"You'll get used to it."

"No, I won't." Charlie leaned forward and spoke with great care. "Try to remember this. I am leaving in November. Do not make long-term plans for me."

Allie smiled at him. "All right."

Oh, Lord. He sighed at her. "Do you listen to a word I say?"

"Only the good stuff," Allie told him and he gave up and went back to the handbook.

ALLIE WATCHED CHARLIE open the binder and begin to read.

Now that they weren't naked, it was easier to make decisions about her future.

For one thing, she was definitely not going to be sharing her bed with him again. She was almost sure of that. She didn't need any more tension in her life. And after all, she barely knew him.

And sleeping with him would be bad professionally. It was wisest to break this off now, before she really started to care about him. Because she didn't care about him. She just wanted him. She wanted him right now on the floor of her office. Except there wasn't enough room. Maybe the desk—

No.

She looked at him, reading the stupid WBBB handbook, that lock of blond-brown hair falling over his forehead. The best thing she could do would be to stay away from him as much as possible. While he was on the air, there would be a glass wall between them, so that was safe enough. And maybe they could discuss the show through memos instead of face-to-face.

Face-to-face made her think of his mouth.

Definitely memos.

Charlie read something that was particularly inane and groaned.

"I told you it would be bad," Allie said unsympathetically. She had to get away from him. She had to do things that did not include fantasizing about being pressed against a wall while his hands—

She grabbed her coffee cup and stood up. "Listen, if you're happy here for a while, I promised to talk to some people. If you want coffee, the break room is down the hall, turn to the left, first door on the left. You can't miss it."

"Coffee is not going to make this garbage better," Charlie said.

"Be sure to mention that to Bill at the meeting at five," Allie said and made her escape.

ALLIE GOT COFFEE from the break room, smiling absently at Mark and Harry the Howler who were talking cars. She wasn't even mad at Mark anymore. Amazing what good sex and a new shot at a career could do for a woman's outlook. Mark looked at her strangely, so she ignored him. She had enough to do without worrying about Mark, especially since worrying about Mark was no longer her job. This was an incredibly cheering thought in a day that had been pretty cheerful to start with.

Buoyed beyond reason, she left the break room and went back to doing what she did best: keeping the station ticking. She picked up the ratings from Albert, promised Marcia they'd have a late lunch the next day to discuss her show and headed for the receptionist's counter.

"Hey, Karen," she said as she breezed into the lobby. She picked up a cookie from a plate on the counter and bit into it. "Where did the almond cookies come from?"

"Mrs. Winthrop brought them in for Grady again, but he said to leave them here for everybody." Karen looked around and then crooked a finger at her. "Come here for a minute."

Allie popped the rest of the cookie in her mouth and went behind the counter, mystified.

Karen picked up a basket covered with a baby quilt.

"I'm in big trouble, Allie, and I don't know what to do."

Allie prayed there wasn't a baby in the basket. Some things were beyond even her ability to fix. Then she looked at the dark circles under Karen's eyes and felt ashamed. "You look awful," Allie said. "What's wrong?"

"I have to feed him every hour and I can't get to sleep in between. I've been doing it for two days now, and I'm afraid he's going to die." Karen started to cry, and Allie took the basket from her, expecting the worst.

It was almost that bad. Under the blanket, nestled in soft flannel, was a tiny black puppy, no bigger than two of Allie's fingers. "Oh, no." Allie shot an anguished look at Karen. "What happened?"

Karen's words came out in a rush. "Mopsy had her puppies, but there were too many, and he came last, and he can't suck or something, and she doesn't even seem to notice him." She gulped in some air. "And I've been trying to feed him every hour, but I'm not getting much down him, and I think he's going to die." Tears started in her eyes, and she sniffed them back. "And I'm so tired, Allie. I just can't think what to do."

Allie put the blanket back over the basket. "Is the formula in here?"

Karen nodded. "And the bottle and everything."

Allie patted her on the shoulder. "Go home at five and sleep. We'll take it from here."

Karen blinked. "I don't have permission to have him at the station. Bill doesn't know."

"Bill doesn't have to know. Charlie and I can handle it until two, and then Grady's in." Allie grinned at her. "And you know Grady and nature. He'll probably have this little guy sitting up and begging by morning."

Karen's tears moved from a trickle to a gush. "Are you sure? Will Charlie be mad? Oh, Allie, I—"

"Go home at five," Allie ordered. "Grady will pass the basket to you at eight, and I'll pick it up again tomorrow night at five. Charlie and Harry will be glad to help. They're good guys. We're covered. Go get some coffee to keep you going until you get off work, and leave everything else to me."

Karen mopped at her eyes and nodded. "His name's Samson. That's what I call him when I feed him. I wanted to give him a strong name, you know?"

"I know." Allie patted her again, back in control of the world. "We'll save him."

AFTER FIFTEEN MINUTES of trying to make sense of Bill's highly original take on broadcasting, Charlie gave up and went in search of the break room and coffee. Mark and Harry, the big tow-headed guy from the lobby, were deep in conversation about Mark's carburetor when he came in, and as far as Charlie was concerned, they could stay that way.

"Just came for coffee." He picked up a disposable cup and filled it at the coffeemaker. Then he turned back to the door.

"So, Charlie..." Mark was leaning back in his chair, smiling one of those man-to-man smiles.

"So, Mark." Charlie kept going.

"So you've moved in with Allie and Joe."

"Yep." Charlie was almost through the door.

"So how was it in the sack with our Allie last night?"

Charlie stopped. *Keep your mouth shut,* he told himself. *Get out of here.* He turned around. "What?"

Mark smiled his man-of-the-world smile. "You and Allie. How was she in the sack? Not what you're used to, I bet."

Don't make waves, Charlie told himself. He looked at Mark's smug face and thought about Allie and felt his temper spurt. He walked back and leaned over the table until he was almost nose-to-nose with Mark.

"Never…ever…make a derogatory comment about Alice again. Because if you do, I will wipe up this station with you."

Mark lost his smile for a minute, and Charlie turned back to the door.

"Tough guy."

Charlie kept going.

"Was she as lousy for you as she was for me?"

Charlie stopped. *Don't do it.* Then he turned around and walked back toward Mark.

Mark stood, caught his foot on the leg of his chair and fell over backward to the floor, taking the chair with him.

"I warned you not to do that," Charlie told him mildly. He looked at Harry. "Didn't I?"

"Yes," Harry said, nodding judiciously. "Yes, I'd have to say that you did." He didn't look particularly put out that Mark was on the floor.

Mark glared at Charlie from the floor. "It was just a joke."

Charlie frowned down at him. "Don't joke about

Allie. It annoys me.'' He turned to leave and came face-to-face with Karen.

''Just came in for some coffee,'' she said brightly, waving her cup at him.

''Fine,'' Charlie said. ''Step on Mark while you're getting it.''

This will not do, he told himself on his way back to Allie. *This woman is screwing up your head. Keep away from her.*

Four

Charlie was still scowling when he got back to Allie's office. Threatening Mark had been stupid. He hated being stupid, although Lord knew he should be used to it by now.

"What's wrong?" Allie peered at him over a blanket-covered basket on her desk. "You look upset."

"Not me."

"You sure?"

Charlie tossed the handbook on the desk, feeling like a fool. "Well, Mark sort of fell over."

Allie froze. "Fell over?"

Charlie sat down and sipped his coffee. "He's not hurt. It wasn't that far to the floor."

Allie looked severe. "I suppose you had a reason."

Charlie shrugged. *He insulted you, and for some reason I lose my mind every time I think of you.* "I didn't like his looks."

"Right. What did he say about me?"

That was another problem with Allie. She was too damn sharp. "Don't be so conceited."

"He doesn't know you well enough to insult you. What did he say about me?"

"His very existence insults me. Can we get back to business?"

"I'll find out, anyway." Allie waited and then opened the folder in front of her. "Okay. Fine. We'll do business. Any questions so far?"

Charlie gave her the one that had been bugging him since the day before. "Yeah. How did an idiot like Mark get to be a star around here?"

Allie blinked at him. "He's not an idiot. He's a good broadcaster. His voice is clear and it makes people feel good. Plus he's great at PR. He's good-looking, and his picture's been plastered all over the city on billboards. He pulls a pretty good female audience."

Charlie scowled harder, not sure why he cared. "So why isn't he on TV?"

"He's really shy." Allie's face softened, and Charlie got more annoyed. "I know he comes across as a conceited jerk, but he's really unsure of himself. He's never even thought about TV. All those cameras? He'd have a nervous breakdown."

"Shy." Charlie snorted.

"Hey, not everybody is as comfortable with himself as you are." Allie surveyed him. "You're exactly who you want to be, doing exactly what you want to do. That's pretty rare. Mark doesn't have your confidence, so he relies on his good looks to get him through, but he's still anxious. All the time."

Charlie focused on the part of her argument he liked the least. "He's not good-looking."

"Yes, he is. He looks like Richard Gere before he went gray."

"Mark's gray?"

"Richard's gray. Mark is still tall, dark and handsome, and women swoon."

Charlie slumped lower in his chair. "He's medium, dark and dweeby." He looked at her suspiciously. "Are you still swooning?"

Allie leaned back in her chair. "Nope. I've been cured. Thank you very much."

His spirits rose miraculously. "My pleasure, believe me."

Allie smiled at him, and Charlie felt himself slipping into lust. Oh, no. He yanked himself back.

"What's wrong?"

"Nothing." He shook his head. No more Allie. They would work together at the station where it would be almost impossible to make love—he shoved the desk thoughts firmly from his mind—but he was definitely finding another place to live. He'd take her to dinner tonight and let her down easy and then move to a motel. Good plan. He suppressed a sigh of relief at being back in control and returned to the problem of the station. "Who's on before me?"

"Harry the Howler. The big guy you met in the hall."

Mark's companion in the break room. "I think I just met him again. Calm sort of guy."

Allie nodded. "Exactly. That's what I keep telling him, but he insists on howling. Which is not your problem. In fact, I don't see that you have any problems." She beamed at him, the Positive Career Talk smile.

"I'm taking over for a paranoid gun-nut, and you think I have no problems."

"Of course not. After Waldo, *anybody* is a step up. And we've been at the bottom of the ratings for so long, you can only go up. Just remember, we're an easy-listening station, and you can't go wrong.''

"Well, that's our first problem. I'm not an easy-listening kind of guy.''

Allie looked exasperated. "You must have known we weren't hard rock when you signed on.''

Charlie shook his head. "Bill told me I could play what I wanted''

"Which is?''

"Everything.'' Charlie leaned back and tried to sound as if he knew what he was doing. "I like it all. The way I figure it, I'll talk to people and they can call in and talk back and in between I play music I like.''

Allie shrugged. "Well, Bill is a lot of things, but a liar he isn't. If he said you could do that here, you can do that here. You better go look at our library. I don't know how much of a variety we have.''

"Well, I'll just have to give Bill a shopping list.'' Charlie shoved the handbook back across the desk to her. "I don't need this. As long as I don't do anything to give the FCC heart failure, I'll be okay.''

"All right. Now, what do you need to get your show started?''

"Nothing.'' Charlie leaned back and spread his hands out to embrace the world, back in control again. "I can do it all.''

"Great.'' Allie pulled the basket on her desk closer to her. "There's just one other little thing we have to do tonight.'' She reached under the blanket and pulled out a doll's baby bottle. "Samson needs to be fed every hour. We're going to have to cover this until two. Grady will do the rest. I've already called him, and he's fine with it.''

''Samson?'' Charlie said, totally confused.

''The station puppy.'' Allie pulled back the blanket and Charlie peered over the edge.

The tiny dark shape inside looked like an undersize chocolate Twinkie. ''That's a puppy?''

''Well, he's small right now, but he's going to get a lot bigger.'' Allie tried to nudge the bottle into the puppy's mouth, but he made no movement to take it.

Another one of Allie's lost causes. First Mark, then Charlie's show, and now this puppy. Charlie squinted at the tiny scrap of protoplasm Allie insisted was a dog. ''Are you sure it's not dead?''

He stepped back as Allie's eyes came up blazing. ''This puppy is *not* going to die.''

''All right.'' Charlie had some small experience with animals from the farms he'd worked on during his summer vacations, and all of it told him Samson was doomed, but he wasn't going to fight Allie on it. ''Where's his mother?''

''He's the runt. Things didn't work out between them.'' Allie tipped the bottle so the formula ran into the puppy's mouth without him sucking, and his throat made weak swallowing movements. ''See?'' she said triumphantly. ''He's going to be fine.''

Charlie sat back and watched Allie work over the puppy, tickling its throat to get it to swallow. Well, if anyone could save an embryo dog, Allie could. He'd only known her twenty-four hours, but he already had a healthy respect for her determination.

''We may have to do this every half hour,'' Allie

told him. "He's not getting enough this way. He's got to learn to suck."

So now he was a dog nurse, too. Well, he liked dogs. And if this was what Allie wanted... "All right."

Allie covered the basket again. "He's going to make it. I know he is."

At least when the dog died, he'd be there to comfort her.

Platonically.

CHARLIE SPENT the next two hours checking out the tape library and meeting Stewart, the night engineer. Stewart looked like a peeled egg and was not a ball of fire when it came to engineering, but he was something that Charlie found a lot more useful: a talker. After a half hour with Stewart, Charlie knew more about the station than Bill probably did. And the one incontrovertible fact he gleaned was that Allie was universally admired. Mark wasn't.

"Allie's good people," Stewart told him. "She gets things done. Mark is just a..."

"Yuppie scum dweeb?"

"That would cover it," Stewart agreed.

Cheered by the knowledge that not everyone at WBBB was certifiable, Charlie went back out into the city to find something to say about Tuttle on his first show. Nothing too controversial, he told himself. No waves.

ALLIE WAS STANDING in the lobby with her hands on her hips when he walked in an hour before his show. "Bill was looking for you earlier. You were supposed to meet him at five. Mark apologized for whatever it was he said. Bill says that you are never to strike another employee here again. Also, don't play liberal garbage on the air. Where have you been?''

Charlie grinned at her. She looked like an aggressive cocker spaniel, her hair swinging like a bright bell around her face, her eyes warm and challenging behind her glasses, which had slipped down her nose, as usual. He resisted the impulse to push them up for her. They weren't that close. They weren't ever going to be that close. "I missed you, too," he told her. "And I didn't hit Mark. He fell over. What do you know about the city building here?"

Allie turned and went down the hall to her office, and he trailed after her, trying not to admire the swing of her hips in her brown jersey dress.

"It's one of the oldest buildings in the city," she told him over her shoulder. "The marble is Italian. My mother and father were married there. The mayor wants to build a new one. That's about it. What do you want me to find out about it?"

"Nothing." He rubbed his hand over the back of his head and followed her into her office. "The tape library here isn't too bad. I can fake it for a while."

"Good." Allie looked at him. "Close the door and sit down."

"Why?" Charlie looked wary as he closed the door.

"I just need to talk to you for a minute." Allie swallowed nervously. "This is about us. I've been thinking all afternoon—"

Oh, Lord, he should have said something earlier before she started making plans for their future. "Listen, before you say anything, I think you're a terrific lady, but I'm not ready for a steady relationship, so if you're planning—''

''Great.'' Allie sank into her chair. ''Don't think I didn't enjoy last night. I did. But I don't think it should happen again.'' She beamed up at him. ''I'm so relieved you feel the same way.''

''Well…'' Charlie stopped, confused.

''Not that we can't still be friends,'' Allie went on. ''And even roommates. I talked to Joe while you were in the bathroom this morning, and if you'd like to stay with us on the couch for the time you'll be here, it's all right.''

''Oh, well…'' Charlie nodded four or five times, his head wobbling a little as he tried to gather his thoughts. ''Uh, sure. Good.''

''Great.'' Allie picked up some papers from her desk, clearly eager to get back to work. ''I'll tell Joe when I get home tonight.''

''Good.'' Charlie stood up. ''Well, I'm glad that's settled. Uh, I think I'll go watch Harry for a while.''

Allie waved her hand at him as he left, already working on those papers. Efficient at all times, that was Allie.

It was really irritating of her.

Why don't I feel better about this? Charlie thought as he headed for the booth. This was what he wanted. She'd just taken care of it for him. Just the way she took care of everything. He shook his head at the acidity in the thought. This was probably just stupid male pride. He wanted to be the one to break things off. Oh, well. Her loss.

He walked off down the hall, wondering why he felt so empty if it was her loss.

INSIDE THE OFFICE, Allie threw the papers down on the desk beside Samson's basket, and sat back. She was really glad. Glad, glad, glad. At last she'd made a mature adult decision about a man, and now she could concentrate on the important stuff like making Charlie's show a hit.

Boy, was she glad.

Really.

CHARLIE WATCHED Harry through the window into the booth. He was talking animatedly into the mike, his hands moving up and down the console like a maniac's. Howlin' Harry.

Great. First he got kicked out of Allie's bed and now he was following an insane person.

When Harry stopped talking and leaned back, Charlie knocked on the window and Harry motioned him in.

"Nice job on Mark in the break room today." Harry grinned at him as he came in. "Look, Ma, no hands."

Charlie grinned back. It would be impossible not to grin at Harry. He radiated goodwill. "I should have known better," Charlie told him.

"Why? Mark didn't." Harry gestured to the console. "Anything you need to know about here?"

"Why don't you give me a fast refresher?" Charlie said, and Harry looked at him strangely and then explained how the noise level on the cassette and CD players were controlled by the red plastic sliding tabs on the console. Charlie did fine until Harry told him that if more than one slide was up at the same time, they'd all be heard, and then began to discuss the three thousand ways the slides could be combined for effect.

"Great," Charlie said when Harry was finished and Charlie was lost. "I think I'll just stick with one at a time."

Harry shrugged. "Whatever."

"Can I sit in here and watch the rest of your show?" Charlie asked him, hoping that he'd learn by watching what he hadn't gotten by listening.

"Hey, you're welcome anytime," Harry told him and then went back to the mike to announce that Tuttle had just heard a Howlin' Harry triple play.

His howl was actually worse in the booth than it was on the radio.

AT NINE FIFTY-EIGHT, Allie took her seat at the production console and watched through the window as Charlie leaned on the wall of the booth and Harry hunched over the mike. Charlie's loose-limbed body relaxed against the white acoustic tile, and she followed the lines of his arms with her eyes, focusing finally on his long, large-knuckled fingers. He had big hands, but they were agile, she remembered. Lovely, long fingers.

She wrenched her mind back to the show. Fingers didn't count in radio. Just in bed. And from now on, they were just in radio, not in bed. Tonight was the first night of the rest of her career. If she was going to make Charlie a star—and she was—tonight was the night she studied him to see how he worked. Then she'd know how to shape the show, how to publicize it, how to make Charlie the Tuttle flavor of the month. She felt her heart beat faster and grinned at herself. She'd be back on top in no time. She turned her attention back to the booth, keeping her mind firmly off Charlie's body and strictly on his potential. For radio.

Harry was shrieking, "And that's it for tonight for all you wild and crazy Howlers out there. Next up is the new boy on the block, Chucklin' Charlie Tenniel. So here's one last Howler from Harry. *Harooooooo!*"

Harry moved the mike slide down and the disk slide up, and Allie heard the "The Monster Mash" come up on the speakers.

Chucklin' Charlie Tenniel? Poor Charlie. Well, she could fix that. She could fix everything as long as she kept her concentration. She was going to make him a star if it killed them both.

Harry talked to Charlie for a minute and then came out and joined her. "The news is punched up and ready," Harry told her, then frowned slightly. "I thought Bill said Charlie had a lot of experience."

"Yes." Allie checked the phone lines in front of her while she talked. The chances of anyone calling in were slim, but she was prepared to nurture anyone who did, even on the first night. "He had a couple of years with a Lawrenceville station."

"Sure doesn't act like it." Harry shrugged. "Oh, well, it's not like it's brain surgery. If I can do it, he can."

"Stop that." Allie looked up at him, exasperated. "You're very good. You'd be better if you stopped that damn howling, but you're still good. And, Harry, that Chucklin' Charlie thing has got to go. We're running a class program here."

"That I wouldn't know anything about. How does he want to be intro-ed?"

"Well, he hates Ten Tenniel for some reason, so

that's out." Allie sat back. They needed a good title. A catch phrase. "Just Charlie is too bland. Charlie Late Night?"

Harry shook his head. "Sounds like Letterman."

"Okay, uh, Charlie At Night?"

Harry shook his head again. "Boring."

Allie cast around for more ideas. "Charlie Overnight? Charlie Midnight? Charlie All Night?"

"Last one's good," Harry said. "Kind of sexy. He's got that voice."

Allie tried not to look hopeful. "You think he's going to be good?"

"Hard to tell." Harry shifted on his feet. "Listen, Al, I was wondering…"

His voice trailed off and Allie was left with the unheard-of occurrence of a speechless Harry.

"Yes?" She nodded at him, trying to be encouraging.

Harry swallowed. "I know you don't have time to work on my show, but if you could give me a few tips, well, I'd really—"

"Stop howling," Allie said firmly. "You're a lovely, warm, intelligent man. Use it."

"Howling is my life."

Harry didn't appear to be joking. Allie sighed. "Let me think about this and get back to you tomorrow."

Harry grinned, lighting his whole face. "Thanks, Al, that's great." He looked over his shoulder at Charlie who was surveying his new domain with what looked like terror. "I'd stay on top of him tonight, if I were you. He looks like he's going to blow."

"Not Charlie," Allie said loyally, but she wasn't

reassured by the look on her new star's face. "He'll be okay once he starts talking."

"That's usually when I screw up," Harry said.

When the news was over, they both watched as Charlie leaned over the console, pushing the mike slide up and the cassette slide down, and then spoke into the mike. His deep voice filled the production room for the first time.

"This is Charlie Tenniel for WBBB, and I never chuckle. I just play good music and talk to people. I only got into town yesterday, and a beautiful little town it is, but I've already got a few questions, especially about your new city building."

Allie looked at Harry and saw her own confusion reflected in his eyes.

"But mostly I just like it here. This is a great place to do a little late-night talking and play a little late-night rock and roll. I'm assuming this city does rock and roll? I thought so. This one is for my new hometown."

Cheap Trick came on with "I Want You To Want Me," and Allie grinned.

Now if he'd just give her some scope, she could move him from fun to fantastic. He had a great voice and a terrific personality, and wonderful hands—

Scratch that last part.

She pulled her mind back to the show. He was really good. Harry listened for a while and then left, giving Charlie a thumbs-up through the booth window as he went. Charlie nodded and then looked out at Allie.

"You're doing great," she said to him, doing her cheerleader imitation through the production mike. It was like being back with Mark, except this time she was telling the truth. "Your voice is terrific. No wonder you were a hit in Lawrenceville."

Charlie shook his head. The song ended, and he worked the slides and leaned into the mike again. "Like I said before, I never chuckle, but I don't mind having a few laughs now and then, for all the right reasons. One of those reasons seems to me to be this new city building His Honor the Mayor wants built."

Allie froze at the console. *No.* Not the mayor. Bill played poker with him every Thursday. This was not the way to build an audience, this was the way to build an enemy. An enemy they didn't need, especially if it was the boss. She tried to shake her head at him through the window, but he was oblivious, concentrating on the mike.

"Now, I'm new in town," Charlie went on, "so maybe you can call in and tell me I'm all wet here, but I was in your old city building today, and it's a beautiful place. Marble floors, frosted glass, lots of wood paneling, and that's real wood paneling not that splintery stuff they sell for two dollars and ninety-nine cents at the back of the lumberyard. This is a building that was made with good materials, fine workmanship, and above all, pride. It's the kind of building that might inspire a politician who worked there to take the service part of being a public servant seriously. Now, if you laughed at that, my friend, you're a cynic. Shame on you."

Allie clasped her hands in front of her and prayed, *Don't say anything dumb, Charlie. Please.*

"So where's the joke? Well, have you seen the model for the new city building? Hey, take a trip downtown to the old building to the planning office and have yourself a laugh. It looks like a one-story parking garage with windows. Which might be pretty appropriate for the politicians around here—a place to park and watch the world go by. Of course, like I said, I'm new in town, so I don't really know much about your politicians. Except that if they prefer this new concrete bunker to their old marble palace, they have lousy taste in architecture.

"If you think the old city building deserves another hundred years, call in and let the city know why. And if you think the new plan is better, well, call in and tell me I'm wrong. In the meantime, this one's for the city building. Hang in there, old lady."

When she heard the beginning of Aretha Franklin's "Rescue Me," Allie put her head in her hands and gave herself over to a moment of panic. Then reality claimed her. Bill never listened to the show, and she was pretty sure the mayor didn't, either. The station had been playing opera for the past week, and before that there had been Waldo and the aliens. Charlie couldn't have more than four people listening to him, and they were going to be mad he wasn't discussing the Martian question. There was nothing to worry about.

Then the phone rang.

"WBBB, the Charlie Tenniel show," Allie said.

The voice was an old man's, raspy and loud. "Yeah, let me talk to that disc jockey fellow."

"Certainly, sir. Can I tell him what you'd like to say?"

"No, damn it, I'm gonna do that."

"Uh, right. Sure." Allie hesitated, knowing she should find out what the caller wanted before turning him over to Charlie. On the other hand, he obviously wasn't going to tell her. And it would be a bad idea to alienate any callers. After all, this might be the only one Charlie got. And it would be a chance for her to find out how he handled himself with callers. "Could I have your name, please?"

"Eb Groats."

"You've got a caller," Allie told Charlie over the production mike. "A Mr. Eb Groats."

Charlie nodded and Allie punched up the call. Samson whimpered at her feet, and Allie stuck her head under the desk to see what was wrong. He actually seemed hungry, and she hurried to drip more formula into his mouth, giving all her attention to him until Charlie came back on the air after the song.

"I've been talking to Eb Groats from up north of the city limits. Eb tells me he was around when part of the building went up. Right, Eb?"

"Well, son, like I was telling you, we put that back wing up about '35. My first job, I wasn't more'n seventeen."

"Well, Eb, you did a great job."

"Hell, yes."

"Don't say hell, Eb. The FCC doesn't like it."

"My wife doesn't either. The hell with her."

"But about the city building, Eb."

"Well, you're right about one thing. That building was built to last. Any dang fool could see that."

"Even me."

"Even you. Even that other dang fool Rollie Whitcomb."

"Mayor Whitcomb seems pretty sold on the new building."

"Course, he does. His brother's gonna get the contract."

Charlie said, "What?" and Allie raised her head so fast she smacked it on the underside of the producer's desk.

"You check into it, boy. The contract will say Somebody or Other Construction, but you follow the trail back and you'll find Al Whitcomb's name on it."

Oh, no, not this. Allie rubbed the back of her head and thought fast.

"I think that's slander, Eb."

"Not if it's true, it ain't. I'm old, but I ain't stupid."

"That's for darn sure. Well, Eb, you've certainly made my first night on the job one to remember. And possibly my last night on the job, too. Thanks for calling. And call back and tell me I'm a fool again sometime, Eb. You sound just like my grandpa. I'm glad you were listening in."

"I wasn't. My great-grandson listens to that fool Harry the Howler and we kind of slopped on over into your show."

"Well, slop on over anytime."

"Will do, son. Good luck on savin' that building."

"Thanks. I'm going to need all the luck I can get." There was a click on the line. "Of course, I've already had more luck than any new guy in town deserves. My first caller is a great guy like Eb, and the first lady I met in town yesterday is the kind of woman a man never forgets, even when she says goodbye, which she just did today. Fortunately, I've had a lot of experience with rejection. Anyway, this is for that lady who said I insulted her in the bar yesterday. Trust me, honey, I meant it in the nicest possible way."

Allie shook her head when she heard Patsy Cline slide into "Crazy."

"Very funny, Charlie," she said into the mike. "About the city building—"

"I didn't mean to, believe me," he told her. "I thought it was just a nice, friendly kind of topic."

"Bill's a backer of Rollie Whitcomb."

Charlie laughed shortly. "He would be. He's just like my dad."

"Your dad backs mayors?"

"My dad buys mayors." Charlie swiveled away from the window to refill the cassette stack. "Oh, well, at least nobody's listening."

Just me. Allie watched Charlie pushing the slides happily for the next half hour, playing music and talking to three callers who wanted to put in their two cents about the city building. Things were going well. In fact, four callers in the first half hour of a new show was phenomenal.

They were safe.

But safe made for lousy radio.

She could fix that.

Of course, they didn't want to make enemies, but since nobody seemed too upset about the mayor's brother, that wasn't a problem. And Charlie was great with callers, absolutely brilliant. More people should know that. Of course, Charlie didn't want to be famous. But this was a civic issue. She had a civic duty.

And she wanted the show to be a hit.

"I'm a slime," she told Samsom, fast asleep in his basket. "A career-obsessed, pathetic slime." Then she picked up a clear phone line and punched in the mayor's phone number.

CHARLIE WAS FEELING pretty good. He liked Eb and the three people who'd called after Eb, the console was brand new and a piece of cake to run, and it didn't really matter whether he was a success or not at this hour of the night. And actually, it was fun. Once again his life was under control. He'd have all his days to track down that damn letter and figure out who wrote it, and then he could play radio at night until he finished the job and left in November.

Life didn't get much better.

Then Allie's voice came through his headphones. "Caller on line two."

"Who's this one?"

"The mayor."

He swung around to stare at her through the window, but she just shrugged and smiled and punched the button that transferred the call to him.

"Who the hell is this?"

"Uh, Charlie Tenniel." He shot an agonized glance at the digital readout on the console. Fifteen seconds till the last song was over.

"Well, what the hell is going on down there? Where's Bill? What is this garbage?"

He sounded like an overbearing, handshaking politician. Charlie had met a lot of them growing up and he hadn't liked them. Still, it wasn't his job to make waves. "We've been talking about the city building, sir."

"Well, stop it. It's none of your damn business."

Charlie took a deep breath. "Well, it's the taxpayers' business, since they're going to be paying for it."

"Screw the taxpayers. You shut up about that building or I'll have your job. I can do it, too, don't think I can't. Bill's a good friend of mine. You just shut up, boy.''

Five seconds. Charlie knew he was going to regret it, but laying low had been a lost cause as soon as the Mayor had started yelling. ''We're going to be on the air now, mayor, so whatever you say is broadcast. Might want to ease up on that 'screw the taxpayers' bit since most of them are voters, too.''

''I don't *want*—''

''And welcome back, Tuttle,'' Charlie said into the mike. ''We've got a real treat tonight. Mayor Rollie Whitcomb has called in to talk about the city building. You're on, Mayor.''

''I'm what?''

''You're on the air.''

''Oh. Well—''

''Now, you want to explain again how you feel about the taxpayers and the city building?''

Through the window he saw Allie put her head down on the producer's console. Rollie must have been right about Bill. Oh, well, win some, lose some. He went back to listening to the mayor tie himself in knots. Public speaking was evidently not what had gotten him into office. His sentences didn't seem to have any verbs, which was par for a politician. All nouns, no action.

When the mayor wound down, buried under his compound subjects, Charlie stepped in. ''So what exactly was the rationale behind the new city building, Mayor? I understand the new building actually has less space than the old one.''

That set Rollie off again, babbling about heating bills, big windows, all that marble, and the stairs. Rollie didn't seem to have a grasp as to why the last three were a problem, he just knew they were factors.

"Anything you want to say about your brother, the contractor?" Charlie asked him when he'd sputtered to a close.

"Fine businessman. Pillar of the community. Mason. Knights of Pythias. Proud to be in the family."

Rollie meandered on, while Charlie waited for a verb. "Does he have the contract for the city building?" Charlie asked when Rollie trailed off again.

"Of course not. I don't know. I don't award contracts. Building committee. Stalwart citizens. Pillars of the community."

Charlie gave up. "Well, thanks for calling, Mayor. I'm sure Tuttle is reassured now."

"Proud to do my duty," Rollie said.

Charlie punched the cassette button and shoved the slide up and music came through his headphones. Unfortunately, it was Paul Simon's "Still Crazy After All These Years."

He was screwed, as usual. He thought about it and began to laugh.

Allie sat stunned in the producer's chair, not sure whom she was in the most trouble with—the mayor, Bill or Charlie. She'd thought that maybe talking with the mayor would boost Charlie's credentials. The mayor could give his side of the situation and Charlie could discuss it with him. Serious talk radio. Maybe a nice mention in the *Tuttle Tribune* tomorrow since the mayor pretty much owned the paper.

And then Charlie turned out to be a hell-raiser. Asking about the mayor's brother. Sheesh.

"You still there, Tenniel?"

She adjusted her headphones. "Uh, no, he's not, Mayor Whitcomb. This is Alice McGuffey, the pro—"

"Well, you're fired. And so is he."

Then all she heard was a dial tone.

She sat back and tried to figure out the probable outcome of the mess she'd created. Bill wouldn't fire her, she was pretty sure. He wasn't that dumb, and if he was, Beattie wouldn't let him.

Charlie could be vulnerable, though. And it was her fault.

All right, she'd just go in first thing in the morning and tell Bill she'd called the mayor.

Then the phone rang and she got back to work.

At one, Allie shut down the phone lines at Charlie's request. By then he'd talked to eleven callers about the building, all of them telling him he was right and one asking if the mayor was drunk. "No, I think he always talks like that," Charlie said, and the caller said, "And we *voted* for him?" There were a few nonpolitical calls: one male caller wanted to know what he'd said to the lady in the bar, and four female callers offered to show him the city and let him insult them all he wanted. "Get me out of this," Charlie said to Allie from the booth, and she shut down the lines for the night.

"Go home," he told her through the mike. "Stewart's here if I need anything technical. I'm just going to play music from now on. I don't ever want to hear about the city building again."

Allie had been working since four, Charlie's show was off to a better than great start, and besides, guilt was making her groggy. She'd done her job and then some. "Thanks," she said. "I'll take you up on that."

She gave Samson to Charlie and told him how to feed him and then watched while he gave the puppy a bottle to the rhythm of Gloria Estefan. Samson was almost lost in Charlie's big hand, and Allie forgot her career entirely as she watched him try to drip the formula into the puppy's mouth. Sam tried to drink a little and then gave up, but Charlie kept on coaxing, his blond-brown hair shining in the booth light like brass as he bent over the little body, massaging Sam's tummy with his thumb. "C'mon, Sam," he coaxed softly, and Allie shut her eyes and prayed the puppy would make it.

She really didn't need any more trauma. She was due for a success here, and Sam might as well share it. "He's going to make it," she said out loud, and Charlie looked up at her and said, "Well, we'll give it our best shot. Go on. You're beat." And she nodded and left the booth.

Charlie sounded even better at home when she was in bed, wrapped in her quilt. His voice was sexy and soothing, and he played a lot of different music including one triple play of Lou Reed, Patsy Cline, and The Bangles, always leading so smoothly into the songs as part of his patter that it seemed like the music was part of what Charlie was saying.

She was almost disappointed when he wrapped up the show at two.

"Well, that's it for tonight, folks. Grady Bonner's

coming up next with some background on crystals and healing and your sun sign's lucky numbers for tomorrow, and he tells me he's also going to be playing some whale songs a little later. Now, for those of you who haven't heard whale songs, that probably sounds like a joke, but keep an open mind and you'll hear music that is truly unearthly. And to get you over to Grady, here's Judy Collins doing her duet with a whale in "Farewell to Tarwathie." Listen closely out there, this is the music of the deep."

Collins's "Hunting the Whale" began and Allie closed her eyes and listened. The song was so lovely that the last notes seemed to hang in the air next to her.

Then she heard Grady's reedy voice saying, "This is Grady Bonner taking you into the hours when the city sleeps. If you missed Charlie Tenniel's show just before this, you missed what he said about our beautiful city building. There are so many old voices echoing through the old city building. Tearing it down would be ripping those voices apart. Go to the old building tomorrow, feel the power in it, and then go to the mayor and tell him that destroying that structure is destroying the spirit of public service in this city. And now, before I begin tonight's discussion on the healing power of the crystal, let's listen to a recording of some North Atlantic whales. This one's for you, Charlie."

Good for Charlie, Allie thought. *He's got Grady on his side.* She felt comforted by that. Grady might be a little strange, but his people instincts were excellent. If he liked Charlie, Charlie was good people.

She turned off her light and listened in the dark to the whale songs, and she drifted off in a dreamless sleep.

She hadn't been asleep more than half an hour when Charlie nudged her in the back.

Five

"Hey." Charlie sat next to her on the bed and propped his feet up. "Did you listen to the rest of the show?"

"Yes." Allie rolled over and stretched a little to wake up. "Now I know why Bill hired you. You're great."

"Thank you."

She squinted at him in the dim light from the window. He was dressed only in his sweatpants, and he was holding a carton and chewing something. She struggled to sit up, and he reached over her and turned on the lamp, blinding her.

"What are you eating?" She shielded her eyes until they adjusted to the light.

"Sweet-and-sour pork. From some place called Mrs. McCarthy's Chinese. Want some?"

"Yes. McCarthy's has good stuff, but Joe won't let me eat there." Allie yawned and took the fork from him and poked it into the take-out carton. "He says it's not authentic."

Charlie snorted. "Sure it is. Authentic Irish-Chinese."

Allie chewed the pork and then looked dubiously at the size of the carton. "Did you get anything else?"

''No. I didn't know you'd be hungry, too. There's plenty of this, though.'' He took the fork and the carton back.

He looked great in the lamplight, naked to the waist, his long legs stretched out on her bed. Allie hauled her mind back to the radio program and tried to make her voice noncommittal. ''So what's your next move here?''

Charlie grinned at her. ''Well, I figure if I can get your nightgown off, the rest will be easy.''

Allie stomped down on the hot little thrill the thought evoked and looked at him with what she hoped was contempt.

Charlie said, ''Joke. Sort of.''

She shook her head. ''Not your next move on me, you dang fool. The city building. Give me the fork.''

''Ah, you liked Eb. So did I.'' Charlie passed the carton over. ''I may wander up north and meet him. My kind of guy.''

''The city building,'' Allie said around a mouthful of food.

''I think it should be saved, but I don't particularly want to do it. Especially if it's going to make people call me that much.'' He shook his head. ''Some mighty pissed people out there when they heard about the mayor's brother. And the mayor didn't do himself any good, calling in like that.'' Charlie took the carton back. ''I wonder if it's true?''

Allie put her chin on his shoulder to look into the carton. He had great shoulders and Chinese food. At the moment, he was the perfect man. ''I wouldn't be surprised. Hurry up with the fork.'' She reached around his arm, enjoying the slide of her skin on his, and took the carton from him after he'd taken a bite.

Charlie chewed and swallowed. "If it is true, the mayor's an idiot."

Allie snorted. "Do you have any doubts?"

Charlie recaptured his carton. "I don't want to talk about the city building tomorrow night."

Allie looked at him, half-naked in the lamplight, and felt a growing hunger for more than Chinese. *No,* she told herself. "You're missing a great opportunity."

"Screen the callers."

Allie looked at him, dumbfounded. "You want me to tell them they can't talk about the city building?"

"I don't care what you tell them. Just don't put them on the line with me."

She looked at him in disgust. "You're a wimp." Okay, he was a sexy wimp, but he was still a wimp. She reached for the carton to distract herself. "Give me the fork."

"It's all gone." He put the carton on the floor. "I'm still hungry."

Charlie grinned at her, and she forgot she was annoyed with him. After all, he'd done a great show. After all, he was Charlie. In her bed. Half-naked.

Turn back now, she told herself. *Get out of this bed.*

Charlie leaned toward her. "You're always hungry. You're the most orally fixated woman I've ever known. Not that I'm complaining."

Oh, boy. Allie threw back the covers and started to get out of bed, and he caught her nightgown and pulled her back. "Where are you going?"

She pried her gown out of his fingers. "I'm hungry. Really. I'm empty."

"No problem." Charlie pulled her down on top of him, and she meant to push herself away, but he was so warm, she leaned into him instead. He felt wonderful under her. "Empty I can solve," he told her. "And I'll make sure you get to sleep, too. Eventually." He kissed her neck.

She propped herself up on his chest and steeled herself to say no. "I thought we'd talked about this."

Charlie stroked her cheek with his finger. "We did, but you look awful good rumpled. How about one more time? I'll move out to the couch tomorrow, I swear."

"This is not a good idea." She pushed away from him and changed the subject to distract him. "You know, you have a great voice. I was concentrating on your body and your face before, and I didn't really appreciate your voice until I heard you on the air. It's incredible. I bet you were turning on women all over the city tonight."

He tugged her back down to him, and she shivered when he said, "How'd I do with you?"

"Not bad." She moved against his warmth. "Thanks for Patsy Cline."

"My pleasure. Kiss me."

Don't do it, she told herself, but she kissed him, anyway, and his mouth moving softly on hers distracted her while he pulled her nightgown up and ran his hands over her naked back. She felt the heat start again, and she stretched against it.

What could one more night hurt?

She pulled the nightgown over her head, and his hands were on her instantly, cupping her breasts, making her draw a sharp breath. She touched him, too, then, stroking down his chest with her fingertips, over his sweatpants until she felt him shudder. He stripped off his pants, and she stroked him again, and she felt his fingers dig into the soft flesh of her hips as she moved to meet him. They tormented each other, touching and kissing and sliding together, gasping small laughs as they collided in heat until Allie thought she'd scream if he didn't take her. "Now," she said finally. "Please, now."

"Wait a minute," he said, and reached for the condom in his pants, and then he said, "Come here," and pulled her over on top of him. "Stay on top of me this time. You'll like it better."

He was lovely and hot under her, and she stretched against him, forgetting her panic from the night before. "I wasn't afraid of you," she said against his mouth. "It wasn't you."

"I know." Charlie's hands smoothed over her. "You just don't like being out of control."

"Maybe." Allie was distracted; he was moving under her now, pulling her hips up to his, spreading her thighs apart with his legs.

"Whenever you're ready." Charlie kissed her shoulder. "Just don't wait too long, or I'll lose my mind."

Allie propped herself above him, dizzy with heat. "What do you want me to do?"

He pulled her closer. "Just ease yourself over me and make me the happiest man in this city."

She laughed softly. "There are other guys in this city making love right now, you know."

"Not with you." He smiled up at her, and she

wanted him so much she ached with it. "Allie, I want you so much."

Allie blinked at him, surprised out of her own thoughts. "Me?"

He laughed softly. "Yes, you. Can't you tell I'm interested?"

He was hard between her thighs, and she rocked a little against him and watched him close his eyes. "Yes," she told him, laughing again at how easy he was to distract. "I can tell. But I thought for a guy, it didn't make any difference who..."

His eyes snapped open. "You thought wrong." His hands were suddenly tight on her waist, as if he were trying to make her listen harder. "I'm going nuts right now only because I'm with you," he told her, and she lost her breath at the intensity in his voice. "You make me crazy. I've been thinking about you all day." He let his head sink into the pillow. "Now, will you please get a move on here? I'm not kidding about the crazy part."

She took a deep breath and found him with her hand. He held her hips so tightly she knew she'd have fingerprint bruises the next day, but it was erotic to have his hands on her that hard. She guided herself over him and eased him a little way into her, carefully, tentatively. He felt wonderful, and her heart pounded and she felt her blood begin to rush and she stopped, trying to keep from lurching out of control.

Charlie made a sound way back in his throat, but he didn't push.

She was doing it all.

"Oh," she said and sank her hips down to his, and

he felt so good that she moaned, and Charlie threw his head back on the pillow and bit his lip.

"Charlie?" she whispered.

"Don't mind me," he said through his teeth. "This is just ecstasy."

Allie moved against him slowly, holding him hard inside her, feeling her skin heat, trying to keep her breathing slow as she watched his face. He wasn't kidding. He was in ecstasy. *And I'm doing this,* she thought. She squeezed him with the muscles inside her and her heart pounded as she watched him suck in his breath. Then she moved her hips against his, and he moved to meet her, and her blood began to bubble. She licked her lips and breathed in and thought, *God, I'm powerful. No wonder men love sex so much.*

She eased herself up until she was sitting, straddling him until he was high inside her. He ran his hands up her body, cupping her breasts, and she leaned against his hands, relishing the pressure there and in the center of her body, and the prickling in her veins, and she began to move against him. She could feel the pressure growing, little flames of heat licking inside her as she rocked against him. The licking flames flared into a hot spiral, and she knew that it was going to explode, that she'd feel him everywhere, that she'd lose herself in him and be gone again, and she wanted it more than anything and still she clutched, just a little, as it began to go. Then Charlie arched up to hold her, dragging her down to his warmth, and she was wrapped safe in his arms as he moved convulsively inside her. "Come on, Allie," he breathed in her ear, and she pressed herself hard down against him and then everything did explode in a kaleidoscope of surge and flame, and she rocked against him over and over, sobbing, until he cried out in his own climax.

She clutched at him until even the tiny aftershocks inside her were gone, and when they were both breathing again, Allie whispered, "I don't want you to move to the couch," and Charlie held her tightly and said, "I'm not going to."

"BILL WANTS to see you," Karen called to Charlie when he strolled in late the next afternoon.

"I bet he does." Charlie stopped at the counter and grinned at her. "Did you bake cookies?"

"No, that's Mrs. Wexman. She brings them in for Grady and he shares."

Charlie bit into the cookie. Chocolate chip with pecans. "Good for Mrs. Wexman. What does Grady do to deserve this?"

"Drives her to chemotherapy." Karen blinked up at him. "Grady does that a lot for the people his mom met while she was going through it. We get a lot of stuff in here because of it. You should taste Mrs. Winthrop's almond cookies."

"He drives Mrs. Winthrop, too?"

Karen nodded. "He helps out with other stuff, too. Mrs. Winthrop came in one day all upset about her grandson yelling at her, and I called Grady, and he told her not to worry, that he'd take care of it. The next day, she brought in a devil's food cake."

"That's what I like, grateful women who bake." Charlie peered over the counter. "Where's Sam?"

Karen brought the basket up on the desk, and Charlie turned back the blanket to see Sam's little black head. "How's he doing?" He rubbed the puppy gently behind the ears, his broad index finger covering the back of Sam's head by itself, and Sam moaned a little.

"I'm scared for him." Karen sniffed. "He's so little, and he's not eating much, and—"

"I'll pour the stuff down him tonight." Charlie pulled the blanket back over Sam's head. "He's just getting the hang of it, that's all."

Karen caught his hand. "Charlie, this is so sweet of you."

"No, it isn't." Charlie retrieved his hand and picked up another cookie. "You'd have to have a heart of stone to refuse to feed Sam." He glanced at the clock behind her. "Which reminds me, I've got to go see Bill. Am I getting fired?"

"I doubt it." Karen put Sam's basket back under her desk. "But you're gonna have to listen to some yelling."

Charlie turned and almost fell over a stack of boxes next to the desk. "What's this?"

"Bumper stickers," Karen said. "Mark's idea. They're really popular. The college kids from Riverbend love them."

Charlie frowned. "College kids listen to Mark?"

"No," Karen said. "They just like the stickers."

Charlie put his cookie down and pried open the top of the first box and pulled out a sticker. It was neon blue with a slash of orange lettering that said WBBB: Turn Us ON! He turned back to Karen. "You're kidding."

She shrugged. "Who knows from kids?"

Charlie started to laugh. She couldn't be much older than twenty-five herself. "Well put, old lady," he told her and she grinned back at him.

"At least I'm not going nuts for a dumb bumper sticker," she said.

"Good point." He folded the sticker and shoved it in his pocket as he turned for the hallway. "Now for the yelling. Wish me luck."

"You won't need it," she called after him. "I heard your show. You were great."

Terrific. Just what he needed. A fan. He was really going to have to get a grip on things or Allie *would* make him a star.

"COME IN," Bill yelled when Charlie tapped on his door. "Oh, it's you."

Charlie folded himself into the chair opposite the old man's desk, ready to listen to a litany of his faults. It would be like old home week, his dad all over again.

Bill looked out at Charlie under bushy white eyebrows. "The papers are calling about that mess last night. Don't talk to 'em."

"Wouldn't dream of it. Believe me, if I'd had any idea—"

Bill flapped a hand at him. "I'm not blaming you. Alice already told me it was her fault."

"Well, I was there, too," Charlie said mildly. "The city building was my idea."

"Yeah, but she called the mayor."

Charlie blinked. This was news. He and Allie were going to have to have a much longer talk than they'd managed the night before. He thought about the night before and stirred in his chair. A much longer talk out of bed where she couldn't distract him. He frowned at Bill, trying to bring his mind back to the problem. "She called the mayor?"

"Of course she called the mayor." Bill scowled at him. "You think Rollie Whitcomb was up listening to your show that late? She called him."

"It was only eleven," Charlie said. "I thought he might stay up that late."

"Only on poker nights." Bill's scowl deepened. "Which I won't be going back to if you don't stop stirring up trouble on the air. He wanted me to fire you, but I told him I couldn't. Unbreakable contract."

"We don't have a contract."

"Well, Rollie Whitcomb doesn't know that. But you *are* going to shut your trap about the city building. I didn't get you here to investigate political corruption. I got you here—"

"Wait a minute." Charlie sat up slowly. "You're going to pull the plug on this thing so you can play poker?"

"It's politics, boy." Bill leaned back in his chair. "You don't understand—"

"Sure I do." Charlie shook his head. "You and my dad. The get-along gang."

Bill's face turned dark. "Listen, boy"

"No." Charlie stood up. "I'm not going to shut up about corruption so you can play poker with the good old boys. I'm not going to bring it up, but if somebody calls in, I'm going to talk about it. Now, you can deal with that or you can fire me."

"Sit down," Bill roared and Charlie sighed and sat down and listened to Bill's tirade, impervious from long practice of listening to his father. It was, in its volume and contempt, the same speech his father had given to him after Charlie had left business school—"I didn't raise my sons to be losers"—after he'd left

the Air Force—"Damn good connections in the military, but you just piss 'em all away"—after he'd sold the computer-consulting firm that had become too fast-track for him—"You coulda been the Bill Gates of Lawrenceville, but no, you don't like the work"—and after any of the half-dozen odd careers he'd wandered into and out of on the road since he'd left Lawrenceville four years before—"Bum." Bill's theme was more along the lines of "Too damn dumb to know your ass from your elbow," but it was his father, all right.

This was what he got for doing favors for his father. His Father, Part Two. Blow Hard and Blow Harder.

"You understand me, boy?" Bill finished, his big white mustache quivering.

"Completely," Charlie said. "Now, are you going to fire me or are you going to let me talk to people about this tonight?"

Bill sat back into his chair. "This is not what I brought you here for."

"No," Charlie agreed. "This is a freebie. And I'm not interested in being Tuttle's favorite son, so it won't happen again. But I'm not walking away from this, Bill."

Bill stared off into space and tapped his fingers on the desk. "All right," he said finally.

Charlie relaxed an iota. "Now, about what you brought me here for. I found out Waldo isn't coming back. You didn't mention he'd shot up the booth."

"I don't give a rat's ass about Waldo." Bill scowled. "I want to know that that letter was bull."

Charlie sighed. "It's going to take a little while. I'm starting at ground zero since you didn't save the letter.

I can imagine Allie doing damn near anything if she put her mind to it, but I can't imagine her as a crook. And Joe—'' He broke off. ''Joe's gay. Could that have been it?''

Bill waved the idea away. ''Whole town knows Joe's gay. That all you've come up with?''

''Well, Mark doesn't seem to have the brains to break any law and get away with it, and Marcia's more likely to spit in somebody's face than sneak around, and Stewart doesn't have the focus. Karen's not the master-criminal type, although I suppose she'd make a nice dupe. You and Beattie have too much to lose. Unless Grady's been faith healing or Harry's been stealing car parts, I don't see many potential criminals here. 'Course, I haven't met everybody yet. I've only been here a day.''

''Well, keep working on it.''

Charlie sighed. ''You know, it would have been a great help if you'd kept that letter.''

''It didn't say that much.'' Bill looked away. ''Just that something was going on here that I didn't know about. Some smart-ass, stirring up trouble. Couldn't even spell.''

''That's not much help.'' Bill refused to meet his eyes and Charlie gave up. ''All right, but I'm not making any guarantees. It's probably nothing. And in the meantime, I have to learn radio.''

''That's why I gave you Alice.'' Bill finally looked back at him. ''After I told everybody you were Ten, I had to, or you'd have died on the air and everybody would have known something was up.'' He scowled at Charlie. ''You owe me for that. I had to promise Mark a raise just to get him to give her up.''

Charlie blinked. "Mark didn't fire her?"

Bill snorted. "Of course not. He's not stupid. She's the best damn producer in the business. But Lisa's going to work out fine. Don't worry about it."

Great. Allie had lost her prime-time spot because of him. Somehow, he wasn't anxious to share that with her.

Bill went on talking. "Just do what Alice tells you to do. And stop whining about the city building."

"Why don't you just give me a list of all the graft your friends are involved in," Charlie suggested. "It'll help me steer clear of those topics."

"Very funny." Bill leaned forward, and the power in his eyes was no joke. "You leave politics alone, you hear?"

Charlie met his eyes. "And tonight?"

Bill sighed. "Don't bring it up. If somebody wants to talk, let 'em." He swung his head from side to side like a grumpy bear. "It would look real bad if we shut down on it now, anyway. Like we were covering up."

"Well, that's what I thought." Charlie stood up.

Bill snorted.

"Right," Charlie said.

ALLIE STOOD OUTSIDE the office and waited for Charlie, afraid the city building was dead in the water as a show topic. Bill hated controversy—page six in the handbook—and Charlie wanted a nice, quiet little call-in show that nobody listened to. After last night, her general inclination was to give Charlie anything he wanted, but this was her career on the line. Maybe she could seduce him into talking about it on the air...

She gave the idea careful consideration and discarded it. Charlie would cheerfully cooperate with being seduced, but then he'd still refuse to talk about it. He was as stubborn as...well, as she was.

Then she heard Bill's voice go up, and she put her ear to the door to try to make out the words. He was calling Charlie a lot of names for somebody who was agreeing with him.

Harry went by as she listened. "Getting anything good?"

"Shut up," she said. "I can't hear."

Harry went on and so did Bill, but in a minute Harry was back with his Lion King glass from the break room. "Try this."

The glass helped significantly. "He's yelling at Charlie about the city building," she told Harry as a payback for the glass.

Harry snorted. "Oh, that's a surprise. What's Charlie saying?"

Allie frowned. "Nothing. Bill's just raving."

"Charlie must be stonewalling. Let me hear."

Allie passed the glass over to Harry and leaned against the wall to think. Charlie wasn't telling Bill he was going to bury the story. So he was either doing it to twist Bill's tail, which would be dumb but entirely in character for Charlie, or he'd decided to keep pursuing the scandal. She sighed and pushed her glasses back up the bridge of her nose. That was really too much to hope for.

Karen came up behind them, basket in hand. "I thought you were in the booth," she said to Harry, and he shushed her.

"Beattie's doing the news," he said. "She wanted to." Then he went back to listening.

"Charlie still in there?" Karen asked Allie and she nodded, trying to press her ear to the sliver of door not blocked by Harry's bulk. Maybe Charlie really was defending the city building; maybe they could run with it tonight.

Imagine the people who would call in.

Imagine the ratings.

"This about the city building?" Stewart said from behind Karen.

"Shh," Karen said as she leaned around Allie. "What did he call Charlie?"

"A shit-for-brains moron," Harry reported. "He called me that once. It means he's winding down. Damn, he's stopped yelling. I can't hear."

"Is he fired?" Stewart asked and all three of them turned to him and said, "No!" and then they all turned back to the door.

Allie pressed her ear to the door. "What's going on?" She tugged on Harry's sleeve. "They're too quiet."

Harry shook his head. "Something about Waldo. I missed it." He listened for a couple of minutes. "They're talking too low."

"Give me the glass." Allie tugged again. The suspense was too great to bear. "Is Charlie saying he wants the city building on the show?"

Harry waved her away. "I told you, I can't hear 'em. They're talking low."

The door opened suddenly, and Harry's glass dropped like a stone in front of a surprised Charlie.

"Juice," Harry told him, hefting the glass. "Juice break. The news is on and..." He backed away. "Juice."

Karen smiled brightly. "The basket." She held it up in front of Charlie. "I was just going to give Harry the basket."

Allie met Charlie's eyes and smiled brightly. "I was just leaving," she said and turned back to her office.

"I was listening at the door," she heard Stewart tell Charlie. "You gotta talk louder next time."

"I'll remember that," Charlie said, and then she heard him coming after her. "You can run but you can't hide, McGuffey. We have things to discuss."

Allie took a quick left turn to head for the booth and safety. "I have to talk to Harry," she began, and then he caught her by the arm and dragged her back toward her office.

"Harry's drinking juice," he told her as he pulled her along. "You have to talk to me."

"YOU CALLED THE MAYOR," Charlie said when they were alone in her office. He really was annoyed at her, but she was so obviously figuring out all the angles while he talked that he wanted to laugh instead. When Allie thought, he could see the wheels go round, she put so much energy into it. He pulled his mind back to the problem at hand. "You punched your ambitious little finger on the buttons and you called the mayor."

Allie pushed her glasses up the bridge of her nose. "Well, I thought it was only right that he have a chance to respond to the allegations."

"Bull." Charlie leaned closer. "I do not want to be a star."

"But you do want to save the city building," Allie told him helpfully.

"As Bill would say, I don't give a rat's ass about the city building." Charlie did his damnedest to look stern, hampered by the suspicion that he looked a lot like Bill and his dad. "Don't do that again."

Allie nodded, the picture of obedience, and he knew he was losing. "So you won't talk about it tonight on the air, I guess."

"Unless somebody calls in and mentions it." Charlie narrowed his eyes at her. "They call us. We don't call them."

Allie nodded again. "No problem."

"Fine." Charlie looked at her suspiciously but she smiled back, innocent. He gave up and pulled the bumper sticker out of his pocket. "Now that that's settled, what is this?" He held the sticker up for her to see.

"A bumper sticker." Allie sat down and began to shuffle papers.

"No, I mean what does it mean?" Charlie leaned on the desk. "Karen said these are really popular."

Allie stopped shuffling and looked at him with palpable patience. "They are. Mark thought up the slogan—you know, turn on the radio—and everybody thought it was stupid, and then after we'd had them about a month, the high school and college kids started collecting them." Allie shrugged. "As long as it keeps WBBB in front of the community, who cares what it means?"

Charlie folded the sticker up again and put it back in his pocket. "How long ago was this? That they got popular?"

Allie shrugged. "I don't know. About a month maybe. A couple of weeks. Why?"

"It has occurred to you that they might be using it to refer to drugs."

Allie looked at him with exasperation. "No, Charlie, that never occurred to me. Gee, what an idea. Now if you don't mind, I've got things to do before you go on tonight."

"All right." Charlie gave up and turned to go. "I mean it about those calls. You don't call anybody. Ever again."

"I'll take care of everything." Allie smiled at him again, and Charlie closed his eyes.

"Somehow, that does not reassure me," he told her and then retreated back into the hall before he let her talk him into something he'd regret.

She was developing a real knack for that.

THE CALLS STARTED coming in before Harry went off the air, and Allie listened as Harry handled them with an intelligence that was eye-opening. Then right before the news, he said, "Well, I want to thank all of you who called in on the city building and remind you that Charlie Tenniel is up next, right after the news, and he's the man to talk to about this mess. If anybody can save the city building, Charlie can, even if he has to work all night. Which, actually, he does. The news is next, folks, and then…Charlie All Night!"

Charlie frowned at Allie. "Charlie All Night?"

Allie shrugged, trying to look innocent. "Harry and I thought it was catchy."

"Knock it off, Allie," he said, and she batted her eyes at him, too happy with the way things were going to care if he was mad or not.

When he took the booth over, Allie met Harry coming out.

"You were good tonight," she told him. "That was

a nice intro for Charlie, but you were really good before that, too.''

''I thought you didn't like the howling.''

''I hate the howling.'' Allie folded her arms. ''Why don't you just talk like you did tonight to those people on the phone?''

''Because usually there aren't any people on the phone.'' Harry snorted, and Allie wasn't sure whether his contempt was for her or for himself. ''I'm not Charlie, honey. I don't do that philosophical stuff.''

Fighting the urge to point out that Charlie had a way to go before he posed a major threat to Plato, Allie followed him out into the hall. ''Harry, you don't have to be Charlie. Just be yourself. I thought about this today. Talk about things you like. Like…cars.''

Harry stopped so suddenly she bumped into him. ''Cars?'' He considered it and shook his head before ambling down the hall again. ''Nah.''

''You could make it work, Harry,'' Allie said, still pursuing him. ''You know a lot about cars and stereos and guy things.''

Harry stopped again and Allie bumped into him again. ''Guy things? Cut me a break.''

''*Harry.*'' The exasperation in her voice must have gotten to him because he turned around. ''You can do this,'' she said slowly and distinctly. ''I will help you.''

Harry shook his head at her. ''If anybody could, you could, Al, but I don't think so. I'm just not star material.''

''Yes, you are,'' Allie said, but he turned away again. ''Wait a minute.'' She caught his arm. ''How's Sam?''

Harry shrugged again. "I got a little more formula down him. Not much. I don't think he's going to make it."

"Oh, no," Allie said and went back to the booth to see if she could tickle some more calories into the puppy.

BY ONE, Charlie had logged twenty-one calls: sixteen in favor of the city building, three in favor of impeaching the mayor and two women in favor of dating Charlie when he got off work. He was pretty sure he'd contained the controversy, but he was also pretty sure that the mayor and his brother had just lost a ton of money thanks to him.

So much for laying low.

Allie waved to him through the studio window. "Do you need me to stay around?" she said into her mike.

She looked tired, so Charlie shook his head at her. "Just shut the phones down. Sam and I are going to take it easy for the rest of the night." He tried to tickle the puppy into taking the bottle again, but it was no go.

He hated it, but they were going to lose him.

Allie came in to check on Sam before she left. "How is he?" she asked, but the tape was done, and Charlie set up the next triple play: Billy Joel, Heart and Tony Bennett. He listened to "River of Dreams" begin before he turned back to the Allie and the puppy.

"Not good." He took off the headphones and put them on the counter next to the basket. "See?" He tickled the puppy's chin and Sam moved his mouth weakly once. "I can't get him to take much. Harry said the same thing. I don't think he's going to make it, Al."

Allie lifted the tiny body out of the basket and put him on the counter to rub his stomach. "Maybe he's too warm. Maybe it makes him lethargic."

"He's a puppy. He should probably be in an incubator."

Sam began to move his legs feebly against the counter.

"He's cold," Charlie said, but Allie held the bottle to his mouth and Sam took it, making feeble sucking sounds, gulping down formula.

Charlie put his head down next to Sam, pushing the headphones away. "I'll be damned. He's taking it. No, wait, he's stopped."

"Wait a minute. Move your head." Allie shoved his head away from the puppy and pulled the headphones back close, and Sam began to suck again, weakly, but with a good rhythm.

"I don't believe it," Charlie said. "He likes Billy."

"Maybe it's the beat." Allie smiled down at the puppy. "Maybe it sounds like his mom's heart or something."

"Well, whatever it is, it's working." Samson sucked on like a champ and Charlie sat back, more relieved than he'd realized. Maybe Sam would make it, after all.

Allie bent over the puppy, cooing encouragement. Her rump was right in front of him. Practically an invitation. He pulled her into his lap, careful not to knock the bottle out of her hand or out of Sam's mouth, and wrapped his arms around her waist from behind. Her blue sweater was made of some kind of soft bubbly yarn, and she was warm against him, and he buried his face in the back of her neck and smelled the flowers in her shampoo. He spoke to her, mainly because he wanted to hear her voice. "How's the show so far?"

"Terrific, as always." Allie concentrated on Sam. "I can't believe this. He's drinking like a fraternity boy."

"What do you mean, 'as always.' This is just the second time we did this." Charlie tightened his arms at the thought.

"Well, we're good." Allie's voice went cold. "He's stopping. What's wrong?"

Charlie reached around her for the headphones and listened. "He must not like 'Friends in Low Places.' It's one of my favorites."

"Well, play Billy again, for heaven's sake." Allie squirmed around on his lap, exasperated. "He *drinks* when you play Billy."

Charlie swallowed and put the headphones back. "Stop moving around on me like that. It's distracting."

"Play Billy." Allie's voice brooked no disagreement.

"Burp him until this is done and then I'll put Billy back on again," Charlie said, surrendering. "Does it have to be 'River of Dreams'?"

"I don't know." Allie bent over the puppy, and Charlie let his hand trail down her back. "Better not mess with success. Play Billy."

"Right," Charlie said, and when Heart was done,

he let Billy rip again, and Sam went back to the bottle like a trooper.

By the third play-through, Sam had fallen asleep and was back in his basket.

"I bet if we put headphones on his basket, he'd do better." Allie started to get up. "There's a pair—"

"Wait a minute." Charlie pulled her back into his lap, and when she turned to protest, he kissed her, wanting her softness against him and her mouth on his for just a moment. She relaxed against him, and he felt her tongue tease his mouth, and then he grinned and opened to her, cupping her breast hard in his hand while he bent her head back with the kiss and she wrapped her arms around him.

"Hello," she said a few minutes later, coming up for air. "What was that for? I'm in favor of it, but what was that for?"

"That was for me," Charlie told her, trying to get his breath back. "Go get those headphones now, or I'll take you right here in the booth."

"Oh." Allie stayed where she was for a moment and then grinned when he didn't move. "Talk's cheap, Tenniel."

He grabbed for her then but she slipped away from his hands, and he let her go because the song was over, and also because he had every intention of plying her with Chinese food later and of making love to her until she screamed.

"THIS IS GREAT," Allie said at two-thirty as they split a double order of garlic chicken, eating from the carton with two forks this time. "The show was really good tonight, right up to the end. I knew you were going to be a hit, but I had no idea it would be this fast. And I haven't even started on the publicity yet. This is wonderful.''

Charlie stabbed his fork into the chicken. ''No, it's not. I told you, I don't want to be famous, so just knock it off.''

Allie gave an exasperated sigh. He really was impossible. It didn't matter because she was going to make him famous, anyway, but he was still impossible. ''What's wrong with you? Why don't you want to be a success?''

Charlie ignored her. ''Dump some rice in here, the garlic's really heavy.''

''I bet I know what's wrong.'' Allie tipped the rice carton into the chicken.

''I do, too. There's not enough rice.''

''No, you're afraid of success.'' Allie patted his hand, suddenly sympathetic. After all, he had hit the big time pretty quickly. ''It's very common. You'll get used to it. Trust me.''

Charlie moved the carton away from her, holding it behind him. ''No, I won't. Look at me.''

Allie obediently looked up at him, her fork poised in case he moved the carton back.

''I do not want to be successful,'' he said, speaking slowly and distinctly. ''Successful screws with people's heads and makes them think they're above the law and can get away with anything. I'm not like that. I am not going to promote the show. I am not going to have my picture taken. And I am not going to ask any more questions that will get me in trouble. I just want a nice, quiet show. I'm a nice, quiet guy, and I want a nice, quiet show. Is that too much to ask?'' He glared at Allie and she glared back at him, annoyed that he could be so wimpy.

"No," she snapped. "Certainly not. Anything I can do to help you on the road to obscurity?"

"Yes." Charlie moved the carton back within her reach. "Give me something nonexplosive to talk about tomorrow. Something nice and innocuous."

Allie stabbed her fork into the chicken. "Stewart drinks coffee from the break-room urn and doesn't pay for it and then he blames the money shortage on the technicians." She chomped down on her forkful of chicken and gazed balefully at him.

He rolled his eyes. "Well, that is fascinating, but I don't think Greater Tuttle will be interested. Come on, cooperate. You're my producer, produce. And move over. You're hogging the bed." Charlie shoved her over with his hip and looked into the carton. "Oh, there's rice on the bottom. Maybe we should dump this stuff out on plates."

"Whatever you want, Oh Great One."

"I want another topic for tomorrow's show," Charlie said.

"Okay, how about…" Allie leaned over his shoulder and scooped up some more chicken, trying to think of something stupid for him. "Sometimes Grady does his show stoned."

Charlie visibly corraled his patience. "I noticed. But I don't think Tuttle will think that's news, either. I need a real topic here. Stop sulking and give me some help."

Allie shrugged. "Okay. The streetlights in Eastown are still out."

"Allie…"

She waved her fork at him. "You said, innocuous."

"Innocuous, not brain-dead." Charlie took the carton back. "I will let you have more of this when you come up with something good. Something people will talk to me about, so I won't get fired, but that does not involve newspaper headlines."

Allie looked at the carton with longing. "It's mean to keep moving the carton away. You know how I feel about food."

"Then think fast." He took a huge forkful of chicken and savored it while she watched.

"Food." She moved closer to him with her fork. "You were all mopey about the little grocery stores going out of business when we took you on that tour the other night."

Charlie moved the carton farther out of her way as he ate. "That's the best you can do?"

Allie nodded. "You wanted boring. Do a nostalgia thing. All we have now all over town are those damn FoodStops. Fluorescent lighting and house brands that taste like dog food." She eyed the carton. "I wonder if Samson would like Chinese? He was eating like a trooper when I left. Do you suppose anybody's noticed we're playing Billy Joel every hour?"

Charlie ignored her, lost in thought, and Allie grabbed the carton while he was distracted. "It doesn't sound very exciting," he said. "Maybe I'll do it."

Allie shook her head and scooped up some more chicken. "You're worthless. I could make you the biggest thing on midnight radio, but no, you want things quiet." She passed the carton over to him in disgust.

Charlie took another huge forkful and handed the carton back. "Old-time grocery stores." He chewed and then nodded. "All right. I'll do it. You can have the rest of that."

Allie poked her fork in the carton. "All that's left is rice."

"Too bad." He took the carton out of her hands and put it on the floor with their forks. Then he sat back and put his arm around her. "Now what are we going to do?"

Allie folded her arms. "You know, we're getting into a rut here."

"I know." Charlie leaned over her. She slid down into the bed away from him, and he followed her down, pinning her to her pillow. "A little take-out Chinese, a little interesting conversation, a little great sex." He slipped her nightgown off her shoulder and kissed her neck. "My kind of rut."

She savored his arm around her and his lips on her shoulder, but she kept her voice cool. "I have to get up and brush my teeth now. And then I think we should just sleep for once. We need some variety. This is getting boring."

"Variety." He moved his hand up her side, and she shivered. "Variety," he went on. "Fine. Tomorrow, I'll bring in a goat. But for tonight, I think we..."

Allie pulled away a little. "A goat?"

He blinked at her, surprised. "You've never done the goat trick?"

"The goat trick?" Allie blinked back at him. "Of course. I've done the goat trick. Thousands of times."

Charlie sat up. "What? I didn't think you were the kind of woman who'd do the goat trick *thousands* of times. I'm shocked."

"You'll get over it," Allie said.

"I'm over it now." Charlie moved back on top of her and kissed her, deep and long.

"Grocery stores are a dumb topic," Allie said when she came up for air.

"Quiet, woman," Charlie said and kissed her speechless.

CHARLIE'S NEXT EVENING began well. As far as he could tell in his poking around the station during the day, there was absolutely nothing illegal going on. The closest thing he had to a clue was that the college kids collected "Turn Us On" stickers. As a lead to an in-station drug ring, it was pretty flimsy, about as likely as a lead to an in-station prostitution ring. Still, he'd checked out the bandstand Joe had talked about before and all he'd found were mosquitoes and mud. No drugs.

He was beginning to suspect that the letter had been a hoax. He was also beginning to suspect that Bill thought it was a hoax, too. At least, he didn't seem to be particularly interested in how things were going. Beattie caught Charlie in the hall and grilled him on his living arrangements, his eating habits and his plans for his show, but Bill didn't even ask him what he was doing about the letter.

It was all highly suspicious, and Charlie intended to pursue it, but first he had to get his radio act together so he didn't make a fool of himself on the air. He shouldn't have cared about that, but he did. He also found himself caring about the people at the station, with the exception of Mark, and feeling relieved as he became surer that he wasn't going to have to bust anybody there. Joe combined the virtues of real friendship and great cooking, Karen was cheerful and extremely grateful, Grady was quiet and kind, Beattie looked at him with approval since she liked the city building and was now doing daily editorials on saving it and even Bill seemed to be warming to him. At least he hadn't called Charlie a moron again, even after the front-page story on the city building showed up in the *Tuttle Tribune.* Charlie particularly liked Harry, who, when not howling, was intelligent and, on this particular Thursday night, in a great mood.

"You're not going to believe this," Harry told him as soon as Charlie was in the booth. "Some woman called in and said she was having an argument with her boyfriend over leaving the car parked in neutral or in first, and asked my opinion."

"That's great," Charlie said, confused.

"No, it *was.*" Harry's face was lit with excitement. "I explained it to her, and then about five minutes later some guy called in to talk about it, and then a little later some other woman called in with a carburetor problem, and then a couple of other people, and it was great." He leaned back in his chair, suffused with happiness. "I can't believe it. People called my show."

"Hey, if I had a car problem, I'd call you," Charlie offered. "You know what you're talking about."

"Yeah, but now *Tuttle* knows. This has been great." Harry got up and clapped Charlie on the back. "Really glad you're here, man."

"Oh." Charlie blinked. "Well, I am, too."

"*Five* people," Harry stood up and stretched. "*Great* show."

Charlie sat down in the vacated seat. The memory

of the bumper stickers came back. Dumb idea, but...
"Harry?"

Harry turned in the doorway.

"If you were going to buy drugs in Tuttle, where would you go?"

Harry's face sobered instantly. "I don't know. I hear the bandstand's the place to score."

Charlie nodded. "I'd heard that, too, but it's deserted most of the time."

"Drugs'll kill you in radio," Harry said. "Bad for your voice. Hard to concentrate."

"Right." Charlie gave up and turned to the console.

"Charlie?"

He looked back over his shoulder at Harry.

"Don't ask anybody else about the drug thing," Harry told him seriously. "This isn't that kind of place. People wouldn't understand."

Charlie nodded. "Right. Thanks."

"No problem." Harry hesitated and then left the booth.

Great. Now Harry thought he was a druggie. The things he did for his father and his father's friends. Oh, well. At least he had the show. It was a weird thought, but after only two nights, he was beginning to look forward to the show. It was fun, but it was more than that. It made him feel good. He didn't want to think about it too much because then he'd start cooperating with Allie, and he'd end up a star, after all.

That would be bad.

Of course, tonight's show about old grocery stores should pretty much kill that possibility.

Charlie put on the headphones, made sure "River of Dreams" was in one of the CD slots for Sam's dinner later, and watched the digital readout so he could slide in when the news was over.

Tonight was going to be one dull night on radio.

FOUR AND A HALF HOURS later, Allie sat propped up against her headboard and watched as Charlie sat down on the side of the bed and buried his face in his hands. He really was upset, and she really did sympathize, but she really was ecstatic. Two scandals in three days. His ratings were going to go through the roof.

"Price-fixing," Charlie said, his voice muffled by his hands.

"I didn't know," Allie said. "I swear, I didn't know."

Six

"**P**rice-fixing drove the mom and pops out of business," Charlie repeated, and Allie tried to distract him.

"Maybe if we had some food—"

"It's illegal." He fell back onto the bed so that his head landed in her lap.

Allie loved the weight of his head on her thighs, so she began to stroke his hair so he'd stay there. What a wonderful night it had turned out to be. The callers alone had been spectacular.

Charlie kept his eyes closed, obsessing over the show. "That one old guy said they didn't do anything about it five years ago because they couldn't get enough evidence. Did you hear him say that?"

"Yes, Charlie," Allie said. "I can't believe all those people called in. Who would have thought so many of those little-grocery owners would have been listening at midnight like that?"

"Who would have thought?" Charlie turned his head to glare up at her. "Did you have anything to do with that?"

"Well…"

Charlie sat up. "Did you call them?"

"No!" Allie tried to look outraged, but it was hard

since she was at least partially guilty. "I didn't know them. How would I have known them?"

"What did you do?" His tone brooked no babbling.

"What makes you think—"

"Because you play those phones the way Glenn Gould played the piano." He narrowed his eyes at her. "You called Harry's show and asked about carburetors and gears today, didn't you?"

Allie glared at him. "Don't you dare tell him that. I only called twice, all the others did it on their own."

Charlie glared back. "Well, that was swell of you. Now, what did you do to me tonight?"

She took a deep breath, and he said, "Allie? The truth."

Allie winced and surrendered. "Well, I did mention to the first guy who called in that if there were others like him, it would be a lot more effective if they called in, too."

"Terrific." Charlie collapsed back into her lap again. "Why don't you just shoot me? I have to play 'River of Dreams' every hour because of you and now this."

"You don't want Samson to die, do you?"

"Sam now eats like you do. I don't think death is an option anymore unless he ODs on formula."

Allie was already pursuing another train of thought. "You know that lawyer who called in about racketeering charges was something."

Charlie moaned, his face hopeless.

Allie took pity on him. It was cruel to be happy when he was in hell. "Well, people called in about other things, too, remember. There was that guy who wanted to know what poem of Tennyson's you quoted.

And the lady who called in when you made fun of the way I eat and said all women should look like the ones in Rubens' paintings.'' Then she gave up and grinned in triumph. "And Johnson from the *Tribune*. I can't believe the paper is sending out an investigative reporter. Isn't it amazing how many people are listening to your show? It just shows how popular you are.''

"I don't want to be popular,'' Charlie said through his teeth.

Allie shifted on the bed as she prepared to move in for the kill. He was becoming a household word against his will; if she could talk him into helping her, she could take him national. "You know, Charlie. This may just be God's way of telling you that you're destined for success. I mean, there are DJ's who would kill their mothers to get this kind of publicity, and you're just doing it by luck. After this, your ratings are going to go through the roof.'' He groaned and she stroked his hair again. "Just lie back and enjoy it, love. This is a free ride.''

"We have to keep this as quiet as possible,'' he said.

Allie glared down at him, exasperated. "Why? This is great. I just don't see the problem.'' Then her expression grew wary as she thought of something. "Well, come to think of it, I might see one problem.''

"What?''

"Well, gossip has it that the FoodStops are mob-connected.''

Charlie sat up. "In Tuttle?''

Allie patted his shoulder. "It's probably just gossip.''

"Oh, no. The mob would be just my luck." He heaved himself off the bed and started for the door.

"Where are you going?"

"To drown myself in the bathtub."

"Hey!" Allie protested. "Where's the food? You said you'd stop at McCarthy's on the way home."

"I didn't get any."

"Well then, where's the sex?"

Charlie opened the door and turned back to her. "You're not getting any, either. I'm depressed." He closed the door behind him.

Allie sat and listened through the wall until he turned the water on, and then she went in and seduced him in the tub so he wouldn't drown himself.

CHARLIE WAS STILL DOWN the next morning. He did snort at breakfast when he heard Mark on the radio introduce himself as "Mark All Morning"—"Well, he's trying," Allie told him—but then Joe passed him the *Tuttle Tribune* and the headline "Disk Jockey Sparks Investigation Into City Building" depressed him so much he only had two helpings of Joe's yeast-raised pancakes.

"I suppose this isn't the best time to tell you that you're doing a promotional appearance tomorrow," Allie said when he'd wiped the last of the syrup from his plate with the last of his pancake.

"In a pig's eye." Charlie stayed bent over his empty plate. "I told you—"

"You were interested in the college," Allie said as persuasively as she could. "Harry's going—"

Charlie's head came up. "The college?" He thought for a moment. The college kids were joking about the stickers. It was a lousy lead, but it was something. "All right. I'll do the college."

The phone rang and Joe went to get it, while Allie stared at him in surprise. "You'll do it?"

"Don't push your luck," he told her. "I'm not going to make a habit of this."

Allie nodded, obviously cheered he was going.

Then Joe came back and said, "That was Bill. He'd like to see both of you this afternoon at four."

"Oh, hell," Allie said.

"Very probably," Joe said.

ALLIE WINCED as Bill glared at them both with equal disgust. "What I want to know is who died and made you two Ralph Nader?"

"Ralph Nader's still alive," Allie said.

Charlie kicked her on the ankle. "It was an accident, Bill. We didn't know…"

"Well, then *shut up*," Bill roared at him.

"Now wait a minute." Allie stood up, determined not to give in. She had a show to save, and for once, she was in the right morally, too. "That FoodStop person bought up half a dozen grocery stores and then cut prices below cost just to ruin the little stores. And when they were all gone, he raised prices and he's been gouging Tuttle ever since. For five years. Anybody knows prices are cheaper in Riverbend, but only people with time and money can get there to stock up. He's preying on the poor and—"

"Sit *down*," Bill said and she sat.

"Do you know who the FoodStop person is?" Bill asked her with deceptive gentleness.

Allie stopped, sure she wasn't going to like finding out who the FoodStop person was. "No."

"Roger Preston."

Oh, terrific. Allie's chin came up. "Well, I hope you've won a lot of money off him in those poker games, because he's a crook."

Charlie slumped back in his chair. "You're kidding. Another poker player?"

"I'm gonna be playing solitaire if you two don't knock it off," Bill snarled. He stabbed a finger at Charlie. "This is *not* what I hired you for."

"Well, of course it is." Allie went back into action, protecting her star. "This is exactly what you hired him for. I can't wait to see the ratings."

"Young lady—"

"And Beattie loved it," Allie said, saving her killer shot for last. "Absolutely loved it."

Bill closed his eyes. "I wish she'd go back to the garden club."

"She's going to do an editorial on the news tonight," Allie said.

Bill's eyes flew open. "No, she is *not*."

"Well, you better tell her, then," Allie said.

Bill leaned forward, scowling at them so hard his eyebrows meshed into one white strip of fur across his forehead. "You let me handle Beattie. And from now on, *don't answer the phone.*"

"But Bill—" Allie stopped midsentence when Charlie took her hand and jerked her up out of the chair.

"You got it," he told the older man. "No phones. We'll tell people they're down for the night. By Monday, everybody will have forgotten. Come on, Al."

"*Wait* a minute," Allie said, but he pulled her out of the office still protesting.

"We've got a great show here," she fumed at him. "And you're shooting it in the foot. Why can't you—"

"Repeat after me," he said as he dragged her down the hall past Marcia, the afternoon DJ, and Mark who were arguing about something. "Controversy is bad."

"Great show, Charlie," Marcia called back to them. "Everybody's talking about it."

"Terrific," Charlie muttered and picked up speed.

Allie looked back over her shoulder at Mark. He did not look happy. She tried not to feel good about that but it was hopeless, so she beamed at Mark as Charlie towed her away.

Life just kept getting better and better.

IT WAS ALMOST MIDNIGHT when Charlie saw Allie wave to him through the glass. He was still annoyed with her, but it was hard to maintain. It wasn't her fault he'd stumbled over the worst case of greed that Tuttle had ever seen.

He motioned her in.

"Nice boring show," she told him, and he rolled his eyes at her.

"Don't start. What have you got for me?"

Allie handed some papers over, and he frowned at them. "Here's the title for that guy who wanted the Tennyson allusion. It was really Wordsworth. And here's the print of Rubens' *Rape of the Sabines*. I forget why you wanted that. This is radio."

Charlie studied the print, a painting of ample bodies spilling all over a horse. "That woman last night who said it was okay you eat like a locust also said the problem with men is that all we look at are pictures of skinny women. She said if we put Rubens' work up instead of Hugh Hefner's, we'd all be better for it.'' He held the print up beside Allie so that he could see them together and squinted between her and the print. ''You need to put on some weight.''

''Good. I'll start now.'' She picked up what was left of the cheeseburger he'd brought into the booth with him and chomped into it. ''You need anything else?''

''Nope.'' The tape ended and he went back to the mike. ''And now, for all you William Wordsworth fans who have probably been trying to call in on our dysfunctional phones and tell me that yesterday's mystery quote was not Tennyson, 'Getting and spending we lay waste our powers' is from Wordsworth's *The World Is Too Much With Us*. Will dashed off that little ditty in 1807, but it's still relevant today.''

A pickle oozed out of the cheeseburger Allie was eating and plopped onto her blouse, leaving a mustard trail on the white rayon as it toppled over the swell of her breast.

''Oh, great,'' Allie said next to the mike, and then winced at her mistake.

''And that was the voice of Alice McGuffey, my producer.'' Charlie grinned at her. ''Usually this is a one-man show, but Allie just dropped a pickle with mustard on her blouse. What's the blouse made of, Al?''

''Rayon. Dry-clean only, hold the mustard.''

''Anybody out there with a surefire method for getting mustard out of rayon, call in and save Allie's blouse. She doesn't get paid enough here to buy a new one. Oh, you can't call in, the phones are down. Well, write. And now a nostalgic wake-up call since it's after midnight, bedbugs—2 Live Crew.''

Allie glared at him, and he shoved the cassette slide up while he tried to figure out what he'd done wrong this time.

''What?'' he said to her. ''It's not my fault you ripped off my hamburger and got slimed with mustard.'' He got out of his chair, stretched and sat down on the counter to get a better look at her. She was actually glowering. He moved back a little farther until his butt hit the soundboard. She was fun to watch when she was mad, but he was still a prudent man.

''2 Live Crew?'' Allie sputtered. ''You're playing 2 Live Crew?''

''Yes, Allie,'' Charlie said patiently. ''I'm playing 2 Live Crew. It's my show. I do the playlist.''

''I can't believe it.'' Allie smacked the hamburger down on the console. ''And I thought you were an okay guy.''

''I am an okay guy. I have testimonials.'' Charlie leaned back to enjoy the argument since for once it wasn't about making him a star.

Allie was visibly steaming. ''2 Live Crew are sexist psychopaths and you give them airtime.''

''Hey, it's a free country. The First Amendment…''

''The First Amendment doesn't give men the right to sing about attacking women. It doesn't give—''

''Well, actually, it does,'' Charlie said, and Allie turned bright red. ''Hold it.'' Charlie warded her off with his hand. ''Just hold it. You're saying I should censor what goes on the air?''

"This is your show," Allie steamed. "What you play reflects your tastes. You have a *responsibility*—"

"I have a responsibility to play music that appeals to a lot of different people. 2 Live Crew may not be my favorite group, but…"

"Oh. Right." Allie was so mad her eyebrows fused over her nose. "A lot of different music? So when are you going to play Barry Manilow?"

Charlie snorted. "I will die before I play Barry Manilow."

Allie leaned closer. "According to you, that's censorship."

"No, it's not," Charlie said, trying not to be annoyed. "I don't object to what he's saying. It's just lousy music."

"But you have a responsibility to play music that appeals to a lot of different people," Allie pressed on. "You just said so."

"Not Barry Manilow."

"So you'll play psychopathic music that advocates hurting women but you won't play pop music that advocates loving them."

"Allie, don't twist this—"

Allie jerked back from him, glaring. "You know what you are? You're just like Mark."

Charlie jerked his head back, outraged. "Hey, watch your mouth, woman."

"You have no respect for women. You're amused by the women's movement and you think—"

"I love women's movements. Come on, Allie…"

"Don't patronize me," Allie shouted. "I can't believe you're—"

"Ah, Allie, have a heart," Charlie said. "It's no big deal."

"—such a yuppie scum dweeb," Allie finished and stomped out of the room.

He started to follow her and then realized he couldn't leave the booth. "Allie, come back here."

Somebody moved toward the booth through the shadows of the production room, but it didn't look anything like Allie.

"Uh, Charlie." Stewart, the night engineer, looking more like a peeled egg then ever, came to stand in the doorway, looking sleepy but interested. "I was just in the break room, and I realized you probably didn't know."

"Know what?" Charlie frowned at him.

"You're on the air." Stewart shrugged. "It's good stuff, but —"

"The tape can't be over yet," Charlie looked around frantically.

"It never started."

"Oh, hell." Charlie put the headphones back on. Sure enough, no 2 Live Crew. He looked at the mike slide and closed his eyes when he saw it was up. "Uh, for those of you listening at home, Alice McGuffey has just walked out in a huff. And for the record, she does a very nice huff. She overreacts, though. And now, let's try that 2 Live Crew again, shall we? This is for all you yuppie scum dweebs out there who dig rap. There must be at least two of you."

He punched the tape again and listened. Silence. "All right," he said into the mike, "seems we have a defective tape. Let's try Elvis since he was on deck next, anyway.'' He punched the next tape, shoved the slide up and heard absolutely nothing.

Then he looked at Stewart. ''Go get me a tape. Any tape. Now.'' Then as Stewart disappeared, he spoke into the mike. ''Well, it's a darn shame our phones are down because this would sure make one heck of a call-in topic. Send in those postcards, folks, and vote your preference, Manilow or Crew. Or maybe I'll try something different.'' He babbled on about some of the other choices he could have made, feeling like a fool and developing a real need for revenge on whoever had wiped his tapes. When Stewart came loping back and thrust a CD at him, he shoved it into the player. ''Or we could play something good like this one.''

Frank Sinatra began to sing ''My Way.''

Charlie looked at Stewart. ''You're kidding.''

''I like Frank.'' Stewart shoved a handful of CDs at him. ''Here's more new ones. Want me to check to see if anything you've got in here has music on it?''

''That would be good.'' Charlie put his head in his hands. ''This is a disaster.''

Stewart dropped the new CDs on the counter and picked up the old tapes. ''Not really. You had your mike slide shoved up so people could hear you talk. That's good.''

Charlie looked at him as if he were demented, always a possibility with Stewart. ''How is that good?''

''Because if you hadn't, you'da had yourself some dead air. Nothing's worse than dead air.''

Charlie shook his head. ''I suppose not. What's wrong with the tapes?''

Stewart picked up the one on the top of his stack

and looked at it. "Doesn't look like anything's wrong. It's one of our old tapes, all right. Must go back five or six years. Maybe it was too old."

"I played it this afternoon," Charlie said.

Stewart shrugged. "Maybe somebody erased it. I'll check all of them, but I bet somebody did it on purpose. Not everybody likes you, you know. The mayor, for instance."

Charlie snorted. "You trying to tell me that Rollie Whitcomb snuck in here and erased my tapes so I'd have dead air? Come on. The man can barely drive a car."

Stewart shrugged again. "You asked."

Charlie tipped his head back to stare at the ceiling. "So Allie and I just broadcast our 2 Live Crew fight to greater Tuttle. All right. That's okay. I can't possibly get in trouble for this. Unless the FCC bars 'yuppie scum dweeb,' in which case, I pay the fine. I'm covered on this. I am not in trouble."

Somehow, though, he knew he was.

That was just the way his life was going.

Stewart left the booth. A few minutes later, while Charlie was figuring out the angles, the phone rang, and he picked it up out of habit.

WHEN CHARLIE GOT HOME that night, Allie was already in bed in the dark. He got a beer, undressed, and climbed in beside her, touching the cold can to her back.

"Get out," she said and drew away from him.

"It's the yuppie scum dweeb. Wake up." He drank a third of the beer in one gulp and then put the cold can against his forehead.

"Go sleep on the couch."

"Oh, no, Alice." He put the can on the table beside the bed, turned on the light and rolled her over to face him.

"You can't for a minute think I'm going to have sex with you." She tried to push him away. "You can't possibly..."

"After you left, Stewart, who has not been paying attention, noticed the phones were down. So he turned them on. We got over a dozen calls in less than an hour. Roughly speaking, fifty-five percent were in favor of you, forty-two percent were in favor of me and three per cent wanted to know exactly what a yuppie scum dweeb was."

"Send them your picture." Allie rolled away from him.

He rolled her back. "One person suggested baking soda for the mustard on your blouse."

"Why are we discussing this?" Allie asked, and the edge in her voice told him she was still mad and not just faking it.

Charlie sighed. "Because we have a meeting with Bill on Monday. For once in his worthless life, he was listening to the show to make sure we didn't do anything stupid, and you go berserk on the air." He shook his head and picked up his beer. "He was not happy when he talked with me."

Allie rolled back over and buried her face in her pillow. "Good. Maybe you'll get fired. Then you won't have to worry about success anymore, and you can stop screwing up my life and the lives of those around you by playing Nazi music."

"That does it." Charlie picked up his pillow and stood up, pulling the quilt with him.

"Hey!" Allie sat up and grabbed for the quilt, but he was too fast for her.

"If you want me, I'll be on the couch," he said over his shoulder.

"I may never want you again," Allie yelled after him.

"Ha." He turned to look down at her superciliously from the door. "You'll probably be out on the couch with me by morning."

"Ha yourself, you yuppie scum. Don't hold your breath waiting. Your brain needs all the oxygen it can get."

Charlie slammed the door behind him, and Allie flopped back down in the bed, put the pillow over her head and screamed with fury and frustration.

Seven

Allie moved behind the scenes at the University of Riverbend campus the next day, making sure there were plenty of bumper stickers and station programs to hand out, that nobody hot-wired the sound system while Stewart slept in the back of the station van, and that none of the cassettes disappeared or were mysteriously wiped clean of music. If somebody was out to get them, she wanted to be there first.

The entire time she kept an eye on Charlie, studying him to make optimum use of future public appearances. She wasn't sure she was ready to forgive him, but she'd been relieved the night before when an hour after he'd stormed out of her bedroom, he'd come back, tossed his pillow on the bed and threw the quilt over her. "I figured you were cold without the quilt," he'd said and climbed in beside her. "Ha," she'd said, but she'd snuggled her back up next to his just the same.

Now, she watched him charm the crowd and felt her anger fade completely. Natural charisma, she decided, watching him lean over the portable broadcast counter to smile at a coed who was waving a bumper sticker for him to sign. Most of these kids didn't know who he was, since Tuttle graft was not uppermost in their minds as entertainment value. They'd just wandered by to pick up those dumb bumper stickers and stopped to listen to him as he sat slumped in his chair with his feet on the table. Charlie's patter was completely off the cuff and off the wall. It took a really focused person to ignore him, and not many college kids were focused on a Saturday afternoon.

Charlie was building an audience. *Yes,* Allie thought and forgave him completely, but she kept her mouth shut so as not to distract him. She had no idea why Charlie had agreed to two hours of college broadcasting, but she wasn't about to question her luck or, God forbid, point out to Charlie how well he was doing. Then Charlie called back good-naturedly to a heckler, and the crowd laughed, and Allie heard it as the sound of rising ratings.

AFTER TWO HOURS in the early-October afternoon sun, Charlie was ready to pack it in. He'd listened for any clue about crime or drugs in all the comments the kids had made as they'd drifted past, and he'd started animated conversations with everyone who came up to him, trying to leave openings for any clue they'd like to drop. After two hours, he'd found out exactly nothing. He had a bunch of drunk freshman fraternity guys hassling him off and on, and while they were easy to deflect, it wasn't his choice of the way to spend a great autumn afternoon. He'd also deflected more than enough young women who'd asked him what he was doing that night. "Sleeping with my producer" didn't seem to be a good answer, especially since, after last night, Allie might still be feeling hostile. Then he looked out over the crowd and grinned. Nope. He'd been a public-relations dream all afternoon. Given Allie's lust for success, there was a good chance she'd jump him in the van from gratitude. The thought led him to other thoughts of Allie in the windowless van with the doors closed and locked. He hadn't seen Allie naked for almost thirty-six hours. That was bad for him. Usually he wasn't this obsessive about sex, but Allie was different. It was easy to be obsessive about Allie. In fact, it was a pleasure to be obsessive about Allie. And the van had a bench seat in back, not wide but padded enough for Stewart to sleep on. Maybe he could get rid of Stewart....

"Quite a crowd," Mark said behind him and he sat up in surprise.

"What?" Charlie squinted at him in the sun. "Oh. Yeah. They're a great crowd. You up now?"

"Yes. Lisa's taking over from Allie." Mark surveyed the situation and frowned at him. "There are a lot of people here."

Charlie stood up. "Well, that was the idea. It's all yours." He clapped Mark on the shoulder. "Have a great time."

Mark ignored him and took over the mike as the last song ended. "Hello, UR," he said into the mike. "This is Mark King, live from the University of Riverbend."

People started to drift away, and for a moment, Charlie felt sorry for Mark. Then he remembered who Mark was and his pity evaporated. This was the jerk who'd dumped Allie. This was the jerk who had probably sabotaged his show the night before. Even more important, this was the jerk who sooner or later was going to try to get Allie back to save his show. Annoyed, Charlie went down the steps to look for her, stopping twice along the way to tell groups of female students who'd asked that he was busy that night. Then he headed for the van, and someone hooted at him.

The bunch of drunk freshmen were back, hanging around the end of the platform. "Still givin' it away free?" one of them said.

Charlie stopped and raised an eyebrow. "Giving what away free? Bumper stickers?"

They all laughed and somebody said, "Bumper stickers. Yeah, right." Then one of them raised his fingers to his mouth and made a sucking sound. "You'll never get rich giving it away, man," one of them said.

"Forget it," the tallest one said. "He's stupid."

"Wait a minute." Charlie went toward them, but they faded into the crowd, laughing over their shoulders at him.

Giving it away free. The kid had mimed smoking, but giving pot away made no sense at all. Not even for Grady, their resident pot head. Charlie leaned against the van and thought about it. If he was looking for crime, he had to find a profit. That only made sense. So maybe somebody was giving away free samples, trying to hook paying buyers later? That ruled out Grady completely since he thought capitalism was a crime.

Unless he was faking it. Unless under all Grady's New Age babble beat a heart just like Charlie's dad's.

It was possible, but not probable. Grady's good nature was legendary. Someone would have noticed if he'd been leading a double life. Tuttle wasn't that big.

"Hey, we're through." Allie came up and leaned on the van next to him. "We are completely through until Monday night. More than forty-eight hours free. Can you believe it?"

"No." Her face was turned up to his, and he grinned at her and pushed her glasses up the bridge of her nose with his finger. "What do you want to do for forty-eight hours?"

Allie grinned back at him. "Watch videos. Eat Chinese. Feed Sam. Make love."

"Let's take those in reverse order." Charlie bent his head close to hers and watched her blush and smile. "It was very cold in that bed last night, and you're very cute today. Is the van empty or is Stewart still sleeping in there?"

"I don't make love in vans," Allie said primly.

"Of course not," Charlie said. "So is it empty or not?"

It was empty.

"That's a very narrow bench," Allie pointed out as Charlie sat down and pulled her onto his lap.

"I have a great sense of balance." He slid his hand under her T-shirt to cup her breast and listened to her soft gasp with a great deal of heated pleasure. "You don't really want to wait until we get home, do you? Think of the traffic."

He kissed her neck and she murmured, "Traffic would be bad," and then he tipped her gently down onto the seat as she wrapped herself around him. "Remind me to do these college things more often," he said as he unzipped her jeans. "I love doing remotes."

As FAR As Allie was concerned, the weekend just got better after that. They rented videos Saturday night and stayed home with Joe and his date, critiquing the mistakes in *The African Queen* and *Casablanca.*

"Bad ending," Allie said when Ingrid Bergman left on the plane.

"A woman's got to do what a woman's got to do," Charlie told her.

"I think she's right," Joe's date, David, said. "*I* wouldn't have left Humphrey Bogart."

"You're a guy," Charlie said. "Women sacrifice. It's their job in life."

He complained loudly when Allie threw popcorn at him and then attacked her that night when they went to bed, tickling her until she giggled helplessly and then making love to her until she lost her mind. The next day, they had a picnic in the park and that night, Charlie dragged Allie off to see Arnold Schwarzenegger's newest exploding-head picture.

Allie had never been happier in her life. "You are one good time," she told Charlie.

Charlie grinned at her. "Let's take some Chinese food home to Joe and David."

But Joe was alone when they got home.

"CHINESE," Charlie called out when they came through the door and then stopped. Joe was standing in the middle of the living room and he didn't look happy.

"What's wrong?" Allie said.

"David and I were spending a nice quiet evening at home," Joe said, "when somebody knocked on the door."

Charlie put the take-out bag down on the coffee table. "What happened?"

Allie sank down on the sofa across from Joe. "Where's David?"

"He went home. Things got weird." Joe looked at Charlie. "Did you annoy anyone lately?"

"Just about everybody." Charlie sat down on the arm of the couch. "I'm not going to like this story, am I?"

Joe shook his head. "When I opened the door, this blonde was standing there, and she shrieked, 'Charlie!' and flung her arms around me."

At least nobody had tried to gun Joe down. There were worse things than being hugged by a blonde. Charlie grinned at Allie. "Happens to me all the time."

"Then she dropped her coat," Joe said. "She was naked."

Charlie stopped grinning. "That doesn't happen nearly as much."

"Then she grabbed me again and somebody took a picture. With a flash."

"That never happens to me." Charlie frowned at him. "What the hell?"

"I don't know," Joe said. "But it's not good."

Charlie glanced at Allie. She was glaring at him. "What?" he asked her.

"Is there something you're not telling me?" Allie said.

"Something blonde? No." Charlie looked at her with disgust. The last thing he needed was Allie getting jealous while he tried to figure out this newest wrinkle. "Come on, I spend every waking moment with you. Every sleeping moment, too, for that matter. When would I be dating blondes?''

"Well, something's going on with you,'' Allie said, getting up. "And I don't like it.'' She went in her room and shut the door.

Charlie looked at Joe. "Is this my fault?''

"I don't think so,'' Joe said. "But if it is, knock it off. You're screwing up my social life.''

THE PICTURE OF JOE and the hooker was on the front page of Monday's *Tuttle Tribune*.

"I can't believe they printed that,'' Allie said as she stared at it over breakfast, trying to figure the public-relations angles. "Local DJ Patronizes Call Girl? How much of the paper does the mayor own?''

"God, I look like hell,'' Joe said over her shoulder. "In fact, I almost look like Charlie.''

"Very funny.'' Charlie came into the kitchen and took the paper away from them to read the caption. "This is weird. They're setting themselves up for a lawsuit here. Somebody with clout must have got this in. Who have we annoyed that has clout?''

"Well, the mayor owns a chunk of the paper, and there's Roger Preston and all his friends.'' Joe took the paper back. "Good thing I warned David about this. He's not the jealous type, but this looks bad.''

"Actually,'' Allie said, trying to look on the bright side. "It might help the ratings. It should definitely get us some callers.''

"Great,'' Charlie said. "The Moral Majority calling in to tell me I'm the spawn of Satan. Yeah, I'm looking forward to that.''

"Forget the Moral Majority,'' Joe said. "How

about Bill?'' The phone rang, and he got up to answer it. ''Even as I speak. Do you want to talk to him?''

''No.'' Allie stood up and carried her plate to the sink. ''We're already on the carpet for the 2 Live Crew mess. Tell him we'll see him this afternoon.'' She smiled at Charlie to reassure him. ''It's all right. Bill's going to know that's Joe, not you, and that it has to be a setup. Really. It's all right.''

Allie wasn't as sure later that afternoon.

Bill sat in his desk chair and swiveled back and forth, glaring at both of them. ''I don't know what it is with you two,'' he began on a deceptively quiet note. ''I don't know whether you're dumb or crazy or out to get me or what.'' He glared at Charlie. ''I'm particularly glad I hired you, you dumb-ass.''

Allie winced at the injustice. ''Wait a minute. The Friday broadcast was all my fault. I know the rule is never to say anything in the booth that can't be broadcast. I broke it. It's my fault.''

Charlie sighed. ''No, it isn't. It's mine. I was the one who sat on the mike slide and moved it up so everyone heard us. She had every right to assume we were off the air. It was my fault.''

Allie shook her head, trying to warn him off. Her job was safe but his might be in jeopardy. ''I'm the producer. I should have checked. It was my fault...''

''No, it wasn't...''

''When you two are finished,'' Bill said, ''I'd like to say a few words.''

They both shut up.

''We logged a lot of calls Friday night.'' He stood up and began to pace. Allie found herself moving her head back and forth with him. ''Even more calls over the weekend. A lot more than we ever have before. And now there's this mess with the hooker.'' He wheeled around suddenly and put his hands on the desk, looming over them. ''*The press* would like to talk to you both.''

Charlie shifted in his seat. ''About the hooker—''

''I know about the hooker,'' Bill said. ''Somebody's out to get you, son, but it's hard to tell who since you've pissed off so many people.'' He glared at Charlie. ''Had to make waves, didn't you?''

''I don't think that was what I had in mind,'' Charlie began and Bill cut him off.

''You don't think at all, son. That's why we're in this mess. Just look at you on Friday. Playing songs about raping women.'' He snorted. ''Making fun of Barry Manilow.''

Charlie looked at Allie, and she closed her eyes in defeat. Bill was on her side. She must be wrong.

''And you,'' Bill said to her. ''You and your women's movements. I've told you to keep that stuff off the air. The only good thing this fool said Friday night was when he made fun of you for that. And even that was dirty.'' He glared at Charlie again.

''Oh, hell, Bill.'' Charlie leaned back in his chair. ''Fire us and get it over with.''

Allie felt her heart rise in her throat but then Bill saved her.

''I'm not gonna fire you.'' He slapped the desk. ''I need you. And besides, you're starting to make me money. Albert raised the ad rate on your show and it's still sold out. Damn it.''

''You can fire me,'' Allie offered, not too worried he'd take her up on it. ''Nobody knows I exist.''

"The hell they don't." Bill glared at her, too. "You're famous now. I told you, *the press* wants to talk to you. Some fool woman wants to do a *human-interest* story on you two."

"Well, we don't want to talk to her." Allie stood up. "I'm not talking to anybody ever again."

"Sit *down*," Bill said and she sat down. "You're gonna have to go on again tonight."

"No," Allie and Charlie said together.

"And you're gonna talk nice to each other, and answer questions nice for the rest of the week, and then when everybody's really bored, you, Charlie, are gonna go back to being a solo DJ and you, Alice, are gonna go back to being a producer, and that's gonna be the end of it. Understand? Find something boring to talk about that you both agree on and talk about it for a week. There must be something that you both agree on."

Sex, Allie thought, but she kept her mouth shut. She looked over at Charlie who was fighting back a grin. He was turning into one hellacious one-night stand.

"Either of you got anything else to say?"

"No, sir," Allie said, and then she and Charlie escaped into the hall before he could start again. "I think Bill has slipped around the bend this time," she said when they were out of earshot.

"Well, he owns the bend," Charlie said. "Let's make this thing short and sweet. Think of something we talk about."

"The show," Allie said. "Chinese food. Sex."

"I don't think any of those are going to make a program," Charlie said. "What else do we talk about?"

Allie stopped, struck by the thought. "That's pretty much it. We don't talk much." She looked at him, appalled. "We don't really talk at all."

Charlie ignored her. "Maybe we can talk about music. You don't know anything about music, but I could talk about it, and you could say, 'Gee, Charlie, you're wonderful.' I like it." He looked at her without seeing her. "But this time, I'm double-checking the tapes. We're going to have music or I'm going to know why."

Allie left him in the tape library, carefully checking his tapes for the night. He might not want to be a star, but Charlie sure didn't want dead air, either. Whether he realized it or not, Charlie was getting sucked into radio.

And whether she'd realized it before or not, she was getting sucked into Charlie. She should have been delighted that all they talked about was the show and sex. That's what she wanted. A nice, uncomplicated, unemotional affair. Except that wasn't enough anymore. She'd gotten exactly what she'd asked for, and it wasn't enough, and she wasn't going to be able to get more because he didn't want more: he was leaving in November.

There it was, the thought she'd been ignoring all week. November. He was leaving in November. And no matter how hopeful she was, she knew how stubborn he was. Come November, unless she did something amazing, she was going to be left with an empty broadcast booth and an empty bed.

She wasn't sure she didn't have an empty bed already. If all they were was great sex, it was definitely an empty bed.

She tried to push the whole thing from her mind and went to get coffee. Her thoughts were depressing, and they got worse when Mark followed her into the break room.

"Allie!" The delight in his voice was mirrored on his face. He must want something, she told herself. He was never that happy to see anybody unless they could do something for him.

She steeled herself for the come-on. "What do you want?"

Mark spread his hands out, the picture of innocence. "I just wanted to talk to you."

Allie frowned at him. "Why?"

Mark put his hand on her arm. "I just miss you so much."

"Why? Did Lisa leave you?" She turned away from him and went over to the coffee urn, trying not to think about Charlie leaving her.

Mark followed her. "Allie, it's not the same. She's not you."

Allie laughed shortly. "No, she's ten years younger and twenty pounds lighter. And it's only taken you two months to notice." Allie turned back to him, her coffee in hand. "I talked to her Saturday at the remote. She's looking pretty frazzled, Mark. Cut her a break. She's still learning the job. Charlie's in the same spot." She stopped, realizing that while Charlie might be in the same spot, he was doing brilliantly. Not a good comparison for Lisa.

Mark moved closer. "Forget about Charlie. Let's go have dinner somewhere and talk."

Allie ducked around him and headed for the door. "We don't have anything to talk about."

Mark caught her arm, and she turned to see him with a soulful look on his face. "Let's have dinner. A long dinner."

Allie pulled her hand away, trying to compute what she'd just heard. "What?"

"I think we should see more of each other. A lot more, if you know what I mean." Mark moved closer, backing her against the wall. "We were good together, Allie."

Allie looked at him in amazement. "Are you kidding? We were lousy together. Are you propositioning me? I can't believe it." She shook her head. "You're propositioning me. No." She turned and opened the door and came face-to-face with Charlie.

"I was looking for you," he said to her. He glared at Mark. "What are you doing flirting with other disc jockeys?"

Mark smiled smoothly. "Allie and I go back a long way."

"As long as you stay back, I don't care." Charlie held the door for Allie. "If you're finished here, we need to talk about this damn program."

"Fine," Allie said, annoyed with them both. Mark had dumped her and Charlie was leaving in November, but in the meantime they both thought they owned a part of her. And she knew which parts, too. Mark wanted her brain to save his show, and Charlie wanted her butt.

Well, the hell with both of them.

"What difference does the program make?" she said to Charlie, and he looked so stunned she felt vindicated. "You want to be a flop, remember?"

She took off down the hall and heard him follow

her. "Are you all right?" he called after her. "This isn't like you."

"You're making me mad," she said. "You and Mark, both."

He followed her into her office. "Don't put me in the same sentence with Mark. What did I do?"

"All he thinks about is what I can do for him in radio," Allie said, slamming her coffee cup down on her desk and sloshing coffee on her papers. "And all you care about is what I can do for you in bed. The hell with both of you. I don't need you." She sat down and crossed her arms.

Charlie sat down across from her and watched her warily. "Uh, I don't know what brought this on, but I want you for more than sex. We're friends. You know that. Is Mark trying to get you back for his show?"

"I have friends," Allie told him. "Joe, and Harry, and Karen, and a lot more. They don't jump my body every chance they get."

Charlie's eyebrows rose. "Sorry. I'll stop."

"No, you won't," Allie said gloomily. "That's how you communicate. Men. The weaker sex. If you were a woman, you'd have the guts to talk to me, but since you're a guy you just want sex."

"Well, then say no," Charlie said, the exasperation plain in his voice. "You always seem pretty enthusiastic when I suggest it."

"I am enthusiastic," Allie said. "I love going to bed with you. But that's all we do."

"So what do you want?"

"I want to talk sometimes." She hated sounding wimpy, but there it was. "You know, really talk."

"Good." Charlie put a stack of disks on her desk. "We'll talk tonight on the show. You'll love it. Conversation and your career, a two-for-one deal."

Allie gazed at him for a moment, looking at the monster she'd created. She wanted to work on their relationship, he wanted to work on her career. Just what she needed in her already bleak life: irony. "Great," she said. "Tell me all about it."

FOUR HOURS LATER, Charlie leaned into the mike and said, "Well, here we are again, all phones working. And for those of you who were wondering, the guy being hugged by the blonde on the front page of the paper is not me. That's my roommate, Joe, and the reason he looks so surprised is that he's gay. Yes, folks, somebody's up to something here in old Tuttle. I don't mind, but Joe would appreciate it if whoever it is would quit sending hookers over to our apartment with cameras. They're ruining his reputation."

"Oh, he'll love that," Allie said softly as she petted Sam, careful not to speak into the mike.

"And now, back by popular request, is my producer, the poster girl for irrationality, Alice McGuffey."

"Hey," Allie said. "Let's try this introduction again."

Charlie shook his head. "You *are* the person who stood in your office today and announced to me that men were the weaker sex, right?"

Allie snorted. "That's not irrational. That's the truth."

Charlie laughed. "I can beat you at arm wrestling anytime, honey."

Allie's voice dripped with sarcasm. "Life is not about arm wrestling."

"What's life got to do with this?"

"What I said in the office was that women are stronger because they talk to each other, and men are weaker and concentrate on sex and ignore other more important things. Like establishing warm human relationships."

Charlie groaned. "Why do women always bring every discussion back to relationships?"

"Because relationships are the basis for life, you dweeb."

Charlie sounded wary. "Tell me you're not talking about marriage."

"I'm not talking about marriage," Allie said reasonably. "I'm talking about establishing warm connections with other people. Men don't do it."

"Hey. I have a warm connection with another person." Charlie wiggled his eyebrows at her.

"That's sex." Allie wiggled her eyebrows back and stuck out her tongue. "That's what men use as a substitute for relationships. But it's not the real thing."

"It feels real." Charlie scowled at her.

"Yeah, but can you keep the relationship going without it?"

Charlie looked at her, surprised. "My relationship with this woman is more than sex and she knows it."

"That's not the point." Allie leaned forward. "The point is that women can survive without all the physical stuff that men need because they know what's important is the human relationship. So they talk to each other. They don't get all the warmth in their lives from sex."

"Sex isn't important to you?" Charlie asked, disbelief heavy in his voice.

"Of course, it's important to me. But I wouldn't come unglued without it like you would."

"You wouldn't?" Charlie sat back. "Ha."

"No," Allie said primly. "As long as a woman is getting her emotional needs met by the ones she loves, she can handle sexual deprivation. But a man doesn't know how to get his emotional needs satisfied except through sex, so he'll get depressed and become irrational. Not that anyone would notice since men are pretty irrational most of the time, anyway—"

Charlie interrupted her. "I don't believe this. You're saying that if we stop sleeping together, I'll crack before you will because I don't have any friends and you do?"

Allie froze in her chair.

"Well?"

"Sort of," she said faintly. "Although I certainly wouldn't have put it that way on the air."

"What? Oh." Charlie winced as he realized what he'd done. "Well, the cat's out, so you might as well finish what you've started here. I can't believe you'd make such a sexist argument."

"Well, there's only one way to find out who's right." Allie stuck her chin out, daring him. "Today's October second, and as you know we were fighting last night, so we can count from there. Let's see which one of us is the most irrational by November first."

"What?" Charlie said, startled.

"You said it would be no problem." Allie shrugged. "Put your money where your...mouth is."

"Allie, that isn't funny."

Allie smiled at him, triumphant. "I rest my case. I knew you wouldn't even try it."

"Did you?" Charlie leaned back. "All right. Fine. We're celibate until November first. No problem."

"Really?" Allie said.

"Really," Charlie said.

The phone began to ring.

Allie laughed nervously and stood up, putting Sam back in his basket as she rose. "Well, I'd love to stay and chat with callers, but I've got to be a producer now. You started this, you talk about it."

He watched Allie leave the booth and then turned back to the mike. "She would pick a month with thirty-one days. Okay, folks, while Allie's hooking up the caller..." Somebody tapped him on the shoulder and he turned to see Stewart. "What?"

Stewart handed him a tape.

"Our engineer has just shown up with a tape in hand. Special request, Stewart? This isn't like you..." Charlie's voice trailed off as he read the label. "Oh, very funny. Okay, here's Stewart the comedian's request."

Charlie shoved in the cassette, and the Rolling Stones blared out "I Can't Get No Satisfaction." He flipped off the sound and swung around to face Stewart.

"So now how much trouble are we in with this one?"

"I'm not in any." Stewart grinned. "You're the one that's not going to get laid for a month in front of the whole city."

"Oh, big deal." Charlie stood up and stretched.

"Lots of people go without for months, years, a lifetime. Priests do it."

"Yeah, but you're not a priest." Stewart turned to go. "Listen, if you need anybody to meet your emotional needs, don't come to me. I don't do that wimpy stuff."

"Thanks, Stewart," Charlie said. "I knew you'd be there for me."

ALLIE HAD HIS SHEETS and pillowcases on the couch for him when he got home.

"Here's another nice mess you've gotten us into, Ollie," she said, and he said, "Me? Wait a minute," but she'd already slammed her bedroom door behind her.

He sighed and stripped down to his shorts, too tired to argue. At least from now on he'd be getting some sleep. There was an improvement. Of course, if he had to choose between cataclysmic, head-banging sex and sleep, he'd choose the sex, but since the choice was now moot, he could see the bright side.

An hour later, he couldn't see the bright side.

He was so tired, he was punch-drunk, but he couldn't get to sleep. He tossed on the couch, tried sleeping sitting up, stretched out and took deep breaths, counted sheep, goats and German shepherds, and finally, as the numbers on the digital clock rolled around to 3:30, he gave up.

He picked up his pillow and went in to Allie.

She stirred when he threw his pillow on the bed, mumbled something and then fell back asleep.

"Glad to see you missed me," he told her body and

then climbed in beside her, rolling so his back was to her and his rear end was warmly against hers.

He was asleep in less than a minute.

Beside him, Allie listened to him snore and gave herself the luxury of one wriggle against him. It was stupid to have missed just the weight of him in her bed, but she had. She smiled to herself and fell asleep for the first time that night.

WHEN HE WOKE UP the next morning, Charlie found he'd rolled over in the night and had wrapped himself around Allie, his leg slung over hers and his hand over her breast. It was definitely one of his favorite positions, and the temptation to throw the bet was overwhelming, especially when she stirred against him, stretching so that his lips were against her neck and her back slid against his front, and he went dizzy for a moment at the powdery, sleepy scent of her.

And then she woke up enough to mumble, "I knew you couldn't do it," and her voice was fat with sleep and satisfaction, and he remembered he'd have to concede in front of thousands of people, letting down not only his fans but his entire gender.

"Ha." He rolled out of bed. "No problem."

"Twenty-nine more days," Allie murmured to his retreating back. "And you're already groping me in the morning."

THE MORNING PAPER had a small notice at the bottom that due to misinformation, the picture in the previous day's paper was not of Charlie Tenniel, but was instead Charlie Tenniel's homosexual roommate.

"Now, this sort of makes me mad," Charlie said to

Joe. "Is this their idea of a slur, to imply I'm gay? It's too subtle to tell."

"It's subtle enough to screw things up with David," Joe said. "He's already noticed that you and I are good friends. He just dealt with it because he thought you were sleeping with Allie."

"I am sleeping with Allie." Charlie put the paper down. "Which, by the way, I announced to Tuttle last night. You have no problems with David. Who's doing this newspaper stuff?"

"My guess? The mayor." Joe picked up his coffee cup. "The word is that the new city building is dead. You cost that man a lot of money. And then there's Roger Preston who is pretty sure to be indicted on price-fixing." He frowned. "You really did tell the world you were sleeping with Allie? That's not like you."

"It slipped." Charlie stared down at the paper. The mayor and Roger Preston were good guesses, but there were also these drug rumors about the station he kept tripping over. Anyone who wanted him fired would figure that bad publicity would make Bill get rid of him. Maybe he had another enemy. "Suppose it wasn't the mayor or Preston. Suppose it was somebody else who was mad at me. Who else would have this kind of clout?"

"I don't know." Joe stood up and carried his coffee cup to the sink. "I should think the mayor and Preston would be enough for anybody. Why did you tell the world about Allie?"

Charlie groaned, remembering. "We have a bet. We're going to be celibate for a month and see who gives in first."

Joe snorted with laughter. "That should be a close call. Whatever possessed you to do something like that?"

"Allie," Charlie said gloomily. "Ever since I met her, I've been doing one dumb thing after another."

"A smart man would leave her alone," Joe pointed out.

"Well, that's what I'm going to be doing for the next month," Charlie said.

Then Allie shuffled out, her hair all tousled. "You know, it took me forever to fall asleep last night. This is all your fault."

Charlie winced. "Thanks, I needed that." He tossed the paper to her and stood up to go. "Here. Read this. Things just keep getting better and better for us."

CHARLIE WAS SLIGHTLY more cheerful when he went on the air that night. "And a great big thank-you to all of you folks who called in last night to say that my significant other has rocks in her head and that men are much stronger than women. And for the other half of you who supported Allie, hey, just wait.

"I'd also like to thank Allie for wearing the most disgusting bathrobe she could find this morning and for not combing her hair before breakfast. Say what you will about the little lady, she plays fair. And now, just for Allie, here's the Pointer Sisters."

He shoved the slide up and "Slow Hand" began.

Harry ambled in on his way home. "You might want to keep your joviality level down a little," he said, passing over Charlie's coffee. "That way, when you get crazy later in the month, the change won't be so noticeable."

"So, you're on Allie's side," Charlie said. "I'm hurt."

"In general, no," Harry said. "In this case, yes. You'll never make it."

"Hey," Charlie said. "Look at me. Do I look tense?"

"It's only been forty-eight hours," Harry said. "Give it some time. I got a lot of money on Allie, but I'm not worried."

Charlie jerked his head up. "Money? They're making book on this in the station?"

"The hell with the station. They're making book on it on the street."

"Oh, great." Charlie slumped back into his chair. "So how am I doing?"

Harry shook his head. "You're a very long shot, my friend. If she gives in first, there are going to be some very rich gamblers in this city."

"What if we both make it to the thirty-first?"

"Practically no one's taking that one."

"A month is not that long," Charlie said.

Harry turned to go, grinning. "Tell me that on the thirtieth." He stopped at the door. "I probably shouldn't do this, since it might screw up my bet, but I'm pretty sure you're going to crack. So, if it gets bad, living with her, you can come stay at my place. I've got lots of room."

"This is going to be no problem," Charlie assured him.

"Yeah, well, the offer stands," Harry said.

Charlie watched Harry stop to talk to Allie on the way out. She grinned up at Harry and pushed her glasses back up the bridge of her nose, and Charlie felt the old warmth that he always felt when she was around. It wasn't as if he wasn't going to see her. It was just sex. He had things to investigate, anyway. He really didn't have time for her. No problem.

"No problem at all," Charlie said to the empty booth.

AFTER THE SHOW, Charlie went home and tried the couch again, lasting until four-thirty this time before he climbed into bed with Allie again, closing his eyes as he felt her body warm and soft next to his. And waking up with her was doubly painful the next morning when she stirred next to him, and he felt dizzy even though he was lying down.

You've got to get out of here, he told himself as he headed to the shower. Dieters did not live at the Sara Lee factory. He picked up the phone and dialed Harry.

HARRY LIVED in a split-level in a housing development full of tricycles and swing sets. Charlie dropped his duffel in the living room and looked around at the chintz furniture and flower paintings.

"You know," he told Harry. "This is not how I pictured you living. Flowered couches?"

"Sheila picked them out," Harry said. "Want a beer?"

"Always." Charlie followed him out to the kitchen. "Who's Sheila?"

"My wife."

Harry opened the refrigerator, and Charlie saw a twelve-pack, cheese spread and a piece of pizza. He spared one longing thought for the glory of Joe's refrigerator, and then took the beer Harry handed him. "You have a wife?"

"Well, I used to. I came home one day and found a note that she'd gone to her mother's."

"Oh." Charlie followed him back into the spotless living room. "Well, she must stop by to clean. The place looks great."

Harry stretched out in the recliner. "That's Mrs. Squibb. Comes by twice a week. Don't leave anything lying around. She throws it out."

"Oh," Charlie said again. "So your wife is... uh..."

"Gone," Harry said. "I waited a couple of weeks and called her, and she said, 'See, Harry, this is just what I meant. You don't even notice me.' And I told her I noticed her. I was just busy. The divorce papers came the next week." Harry shook his head. "I still think it was a mistake. And who knows, she might be back."

"Well, sure," Charlie said, still lost. "How long has she been gone?"

Harry frowned, counting back. "Uh, thirteen years."

Charlie stared at him for a minute, trying to decide if he was kidding or not. With Harry, it was hard to tell. "No offense, Harry, but if I were you, I'd make a contingency plan."

"I'm thinking about it." Harry stretched out in his chair, obviously a happy man. "What about you and Allie?"

"What about us?" Charlie said guardedly.

"You still leaving in November?"

"Yep." Charlie drank his beer. "What do you do for dinner around here?"

"Order out," Harry said. "You want pizza, burgers, or Chinese?"

"Not Chinese," Charlie said. "Anything but Chinese."

CHARLIE DECIDED that the only way to stay sane was to stay away from Allie. The bet was an excellent idea since he was leaving in November, anyway, so all he had to do was avoid her for the rest of the month, kiss her goodbye on November first, and leave her with great memories. At least he hoped her memories were great.

His were phenomenal.

But that way lay madness, so he deliberately shut her out of his mind and avoided her for the rest of the week, waving to her from the booth and making sure any conferences they had were in public. In his free time, he tried to track down the drug rumor and find out who'd sabotaged his tapes. The favorite for the last one was Mark, and Charlie would have loved to pin the drug charge on him, too—those were awfully expensive suits he was wearing on a DJ's salary—but he couldn't see Mark as the brains of a drug ring. Actually, he couldn't see Mark as the brains of a Jell-O ring.

When Saturday came, he took a day off from detecting and went fishing with Harry at Grady's.

It was really too late in the year to fish, but as Harry pointed out, catching fish wasn't that important, anyway. Grady's was just a good place to unwind. They had to take their own beer because Grady's place was nonalcoholic, but other than that, it was a bachelor's paradise.

Grady lived outside Tuttle on several acres of deliberate wilderness in a geodesic dome he'd built himself. "My father thought I was nuts," Grady told Charlie as he showed him around. "Now I think he kind of likes it. My mom thinks it's great." The interior was all natural wood and windows, and aside from a disquieting lack of corners, it was a very comfortable place, full of old, mismatched furniture and state-of-the-art computer and stereo equipment.

"Great setup," Charlie said, looking it over.

"My mom bought that stuff for me," Grady said. "She says I'm tough to buy for, so if I want something, she goes all out." He gazed around his dome lovingly. "It's a great place." Then he smiled at Charlie. "Come out anytime. Don't wait for Harry to bring you."

"Thanks," Charlie said, but then he stopped, distracted by what he saw out the window. Hidden from the driveway by the dome and a stand of trees but in clear view from Grady's back windows, was the biggest field of marijuana Charlie had ever seen. "Nice crop," he told Grady.

Grady shrugged. "Personal use."

You must have a habit the size of Texas, Charlie thought. If somebody was dealing drugs at the station, Grady had just moved up to the number-one suspect. But if he was doing it, what was he doing with the money? Aside from his stereo and computer, his place was furnished with hand-me-downs and Grady himself dressed like a bag lady. Charlie knew he was going to have to investigate it, but he hated the idea that it might be Grady. Grady was a truly nice guy.

But nice guy or not, if he was the problem, he was going down for it. That was what Charlie had come for. He spared a thought for Bill who would not be happy if his only son was busted, and then shoved the thought aside. He really didn't believe Grady was building a drug empire in Tuttle. Grady didn't believe in capitalism. He wasn't even sure Grady believed in money.

Harry came in the back door with two poles. "You ready?"

"Yep," Charlie said. "Lead me to them."

"Too bad Allie couldn't be here," Grady said. "She loves to fish."

"Yeah," Charlie said, shoving her firmly from his mind. "Too bad."

AFTER A WEEK at Harry's, Charlie was ready to crawl back to Allie on his hands and knees. And he'd have done it, too, if it had only been his honor at stake.

But the honor of all mankind?

Still, watching her sit outside the booth was torture. She had her hair yanked back in a ponytail, which made her face more moonlike than usual, and there were bags under her eyes as if she hadn't been sleeping, and she wasn't wearing any makeup for some reason, and he'd never wanted a woman more in his life. If he could have, he'd have taken her there on the production desk.

He closed his eyes at the thought of Allie round and warm, moving under him, his mouth on hers capturing her moans. Or Allie on top of him, her tongue caught between her teeth as she bore down on him, and his hand on the back of her neck bringing her mouth down to his. Or Allie sitting on the edge of the desk, her legs wrapped around him, her back arching her hips into him. Or—

The silence in his ears brought him back with a start, and he said something inane into the mike and punched in the next three songs. Then he took off his headphones and went out to see her.

"You look tired." He sat on the edge of the desk next to her chair, using every ounce of self-control he had not to touch her. "You okay?"

"Yeah." She leaned back in her chair and stretched as if her muscles ached, and he watched her breasts move under her sweater and restrained himself from leaping on her but not from imagining leaping on her. "I miss you," she said, and he snapped back to attention. "I miss you in my bed."

"I miss you, too," he told her when he had his breath back. "But I can't climb in your bed and just sleep with you. It drives me crazy standing up fully clothed in public with you."

"Really?" Her face folded into a smile, and he watched the lines there and reminded himself not to trace them with his finger. "That's nice," she said. "Thank you."

"You're welcome." The line of her cheek was so smooth. His hand went out, independent of his brain, and cupped her cheek, and she leaned into his palm, and he found himself moving toward her mouth, the lust to taste her as inescapable as gravity.

And then his lips were on hers, and her mouth was warm and hot and sweet, and her lower lip slid against his tongue, and his entire being was in his mouth, finding her, at last.

ALLIE SAT stunned as he kissed her, her head heavy on her neck, falling helplessly into him as his mouth moved on hers. His hand was gentle on her cheek, and he breathed into her mouth and she lived in his heat, moving her lips against his, letting the dizziness take her like a drug. And then he touched her lips with his tongue, and the air left her lungs as she sighed with surrender, only to gasp when he licked farther into her mouth, tangling with her tongue. She felt his kiss everywhere, in her breasts and her stomach and hotly between her legs, and she pressed her mouth back against his, spurred by the moan he made as she invaded his mouth.

Then he pulled back, his breath coming heavily, and said, "I can't stand this." He kissed her hard once, quickly, and moved away from her, back into the booth, while she leaned on the desk and tried to breathe.

"I'm sorry," he said over the mike when the door was closed behind him. "I didn't mean to. I just couldn't—"

"I'm not sorry," she told him. "But, oh, God, Charlie—"

"Go home," he said, and there was an edge in his voice. "Go home. The rest is just music. I can't talk to you anymore tonight. I can't talk to anybody. Go home."

AFTER A WEEK AND A HALF of sleeping without Charlie, Allie was ready to surrender. It wasn't the sex she missed so much, although she missed that so much she ached with it, it was Charlie. Charlie warm and laughing and safe and just there. She couldn't even face Chinese food anymore without getting turned on and feeling lonely.

They'd fought amiably over the end of *Casablanca* for that night's program, and then Allie left the booth, and Charlie put "River of Dreams" on and she watched as he cuddled Sam to his chest and began to feed him. Sam was growing like a horse, getting into everything, and she'd caught Charlie lecturing him earlier about chewing on electrical cords. They'd looked so funny, the tiny puppy looking up earnestly from Charlie's big hand, and Charlie scowling down at Sam, reasoning with him about electrocution, that she had to laugh. Charlie had looked up and grinned at her, and his grin hit her like a punch to the stomach.

She missed him.

This was a bad emotion, so she squelched it and went back to work, looking up again only when Charlie introduced a play for insomniacs. She could see Sam scampering over the console and Charlie reaching for him, tucking the squirming puppy under his chin while he punched up the next song. Then the Disney lullaby "Baby Mine" came up and he began to rock and pat Sam until the puppy curled up on his chest and went to sleep.

Watching a man pat a puppy was no reason to fall in love.

But she did, anyway, much against her better judgment and her will and her common sense. *Not this,* she thought. *Not him.* But there it was.

The phone rang and she grabbed it, grateful for anything that distracted her from this new disaster. She didn't want to be in love with anybody, especially not with Charlie I'm-Leaving-In-November Tenniel, especially not like this.

"Charlie All Night," she said into the receiver, and the caller said, "Yeah, let me talk to Charlie. I'm Doug."

The song ended and Allie said, "You have a caller. It's Doug, on one," and punched it in.

Charlie shifted Sam to his shoulder and spoke into the microphone. "Hey, Doug, what's up?"

"Well, that's what I was going to ask you. We were kind of wondering here why you keep playing 'River of Dreams' so much, and now a lullaby? We'd heard your station was wired, but this is weird."

She saw Charlie sit up. "Wired?"

"Well, you know. What gives? You a Billy Joel freak?"

Charlie relaxed a little. "Not me. We've got a puppy here at the station who wasn't doing too well at eating until we put on 'River of Dreams.' He really likes the rhythm. He's doing pretty good now, but we still play it once a night so he feels at home."

"You're kidding. You got a dog there?"

Allie watched Charlie look down at Samson and grin. "Well, you could stretch it and call Sam a dog, I guess. He's more like a Twinkie with paws and an appetite. And he was tearing up the booth a minute ago, so I put the lullaby on. Knocked him right out."

"Try 'Sweet Baby James,' man," Doug said. "My kid goes right to sleep when we play that."

"Great idea." Charlie moved Sam farther up on his shoulder and patted him as he stirred. "Maybe we should play a lullaby every night about this time. Put any kid who's fighting it to sleep.''

Charlie talked on with Doug about rock lullabies, and Allie watched him, hopeless with love, until a nasty thought intruded.

He'd just announced the station had a dog to the listening public.

Bill didn't know the station had a dog. Beattie didn't even know.

They were in for another meeting.

And she couldn't even go home and crawl into bed with Charlie and talk about it.

Charlie punched up a song and continued to talk to Doug off the air, and Allie took her glasses off and put her head down on her desk and tried to figure out how her life had gotten so screwed up when she'd been doing all the right things.

BILL TRIED to throw his usual fit about Sam, but Charlie knocked him off-balance by bringing the puppy to the meeting.

"Good little dog," Bill said gruffly when he met Sam. "Probably good publicity. What the hell, let him stay."

"How did you know he'd say that?" Allie asked him when they'd escaped unscathed.

"Grady tipped me off," he told her. "Evidently, Bill's a sucker for dogs. Grady told me as long as Sam was in the room, Bill would fold."

"Well, good for Grady," Allie said.

Charlie lifted Sam up in front of his face and said, "You're in, kid, don't screw up," and when Sam licked Charlie's nose, he laughed. He laughed a lot more when Sam became the new Flavor of the Week after his picture showed up in the paper, and the local animal shelter called and asked to begin a This-Dog-Needs-A-Home segment the next week on Charlie's show.

They did still have a few problems. Somebody was still sabotaging the show, one night making crank calls that tied up the phone lines, the next swiping the ad tapes for the night. Charlie coped with all of it and avoided Allie like the plague, missing her so much that he couldn't sleep at night, telling himself that once November came and he was out of town, she'd just be a pleasant memory.

He kept telling himself that, but he didn't believe it. And it was getting harder and harder to stay away from her.

Charlie walked into the booth on Friday night, two days after he'd blown Sam's cover, grouchy because he was in a booth and Allie was ten feet away on the other side of a glass wall wearing a pink sweater that made him crazy.

Once inside the booth, though, he stopped in his tracks. "What is that god-awful smell?"

"Well." Harry leaned back in his chair. "It seems Mark got a dog."

"What?"

"A dog," Harry said. "At the pound. A Doberman-mix puppy. A man's dog. Called him King."

Charlie sat down on the edge of the console. "I don't believe this."

"And he brought King into the booth with him this morning so he could broadcast with him. Like we do with Samson. And after three hours, King scratched at the door to be let out.''

Charlie snorted. ''King obviously has a lot of stamina. I'd have been clawing at the door a lot sooner if I was trapped in a booth with Mark.''

''But Mark ignored him, so King…uh, pooped.''

Charlie grinned. ''And then?''

''Mark yelled at him and scared him.'' Harry fought back a grin. ''So King pooped again.''

Charlie's grin widened. ''Mark is an idiot.''

''So then Mark waved the script at him, and King—''

''Pooped again.'' Charlie started to laugh.

''Then Marcia came in and threw a fit because of all the poop in the booth and because Mark was mistreating a puppy. She gave him ten minutes to get the booth clean, and she took the dog away from him.''

Charlie looked alarmed. ''Not back to the pound?''

Harry shook his head. ''Nah. She said she needed a watchdog. She took the dog outside and calmed it down, and then brought it back inside with her until her show was done.''

''Good for Marcia. Although I can't picture her with a dog named King.''

''Dorothy,'' Harry said. ''The dog's name is now Dorothy. Mark missed a few details, as usual.''

''You're kidding.'' Charlie closed his eyes. ''What a dweeb. So then he cleaned up the booth—''

Harry snorted. ''Fat chance. He made Lisa do it.''

''Oh, great.'' Charlie shook his head. ''Wait'll I tell Allie. She's not going to believe this.''

''And then Lisa sprayed the place with that stinking pine disinfectant…''

Charlie nodded. "Which explains why this place smells like—"

"—somebody pooped a pine tree," Harry finished.

"Sounds like a good time to do a remote," Charlie said.

"I've been spending a lot of time out of here," Harry said. "Thank God I don't have a date tonight. This would not be an easy smell to explain."

"Pooped Pine, the cologne of Kings," Charlie said and they both started to laugh.

Allie came into the booth, and they stopped. "What's so funny?" she asked them. "And what is that horrible smell?"

Harry and Charlie looked at each other for a moment and then they both broke up again.

THE ONLY PROBLEM was that since the booth reeked, Charlie had to spend most of his time out of it. With Allie. He was supposed to be talking about the ads for the rest of the show, but Allie was wearing a silky pink sweater, and her curves were right there in front of him. She was saying something, but he couldn't hear because of the rushing in his ears.

He had to touch her. Touching was not sex. Touching was just touching. "What we need here is a definition of sex," Charlie said. "The bet said no sex. It didn't say no kissing." He took a deep breath. "I want to touch you."

Allie flushed pink and Charlie felt dizzy. Usually when she blushed like that, it was because he was moving his hands on her. He thought of the nights he'd had with her the week before and thrown away, not memorizing every second of what it was like to touch her. How he hadn't concentrated on the feel of his tongue against her skin, the slide of her body against his as she arched against him, the heat and the wet and the—

"Oh, God," he said. "I really need to touch you."

Eight

Allie sat across from him and tried to control her breathing. *I really need to touch you.* He was making her insane over this stupid bet. If he wanted her, all he had to do was say, "You win."

Of course, all she had to do was say, "You win," and she could have him back. She could slide her hands down his back, bite into the muscle on his shoulder, lick her way into his mouth, arch her aching body into his hardness, and dear God, find some surcease for this endless need that was driving her crazy. She bit her lip to keep from saying it out loud.

And if she did that, he'd touch her like only Charlie could touch her, his hands on her breasts, hot and teasing, his mouth, moving lower...

She drew a breath, suddenly light-headed from not breathing before, suddenly wanting his mouth more than anything in the world. Her breasts felt hot and tight and made her crave his touch even more, and she moved her hands to press against them, trying to ease the itch and the throbbing there.

And Charlie said, "Don't do that, please don't do that," and she said, "You do it. I can't stand it anymore."

He got up slowly and came to her, and she stood

and put her head on his shoulder. He finally touched her, smoothly his palms lightly over her breasts at first, then pressing against her, and then finally lowering his head to bite her gently through her sweater, and that's when she dug her fingers into his shoulders and cried out.

He kissed her then, licking into her mouth, and the relief was like drowning. She arched against him, feeling how hard he was against her stomach, and his hands pressed her breasts in exquisite relief while every cell in her body throbbed for him. She laced her fingers in his hair and pulled his mouth harder against hers, trying to drink him in, biting his lip, and his leg went between hers as he bent her back against the production table, moving against her, while she wrapped herself around him as tightly as she could.

He was heavy on top of her, wonderfully heavy, and she stretched up to him, trying to meld with him, using his weight to satiate her need to have him inside her. His lips were on her throat as his hands pulled her sweater down off her shoulders, and his tongue licked deep into her cleavage. She scraped her nails down his back and throbbed against him. He pulled her bra off her breast, and his mouth found her, hot and wet, and he sucked hard, and she cried out and tightened against him, blind with need. He shoved her skirt up and moved his hand between her legs, pressing against the nylon there, his fingers sliding under the elastic.

"Wait," she breathed. "You, too."

And he said, "No, this is just for you."

She moved away from his hand. "No." She pulled his head up to look into his eyes, and they both shook with passion. "No. Not unless it's for both of us. It has to be both of us."

"It is," he told her. "I love watching you come." His eyes were hot, and she wanted to drink them in with the rest of him and make them part of her, but she wanted him with her, too. They were in this together. They were in everything together.

"No." Allie drew a long, shuddering breath. "No. I want you so much I'm dying from it. But that's just sex. No. Both of us or nothing."

Charlie closed his eyes, and she slid out from under him, memorizing the feel of him as she did.

Charlie leaned on the table, gripping the edge, his biceps taut from tension. "We could end this damn bet by mutual consent. We could both give in."

Allie leaned back against the table, getting her breath under control while she tried to figure out why that was such a bad idea. It should have been a good idea. "Is that what you want?"

"It should be what I want." Charlie stood up and tipped his head back, staring at the ceiling instead of her. "I don't know why I'm so sold on this damn bet. It's making me insane."

"It's making us different," Allie said, and she knew that was why she'd pulled away. In the beginning, she and Charlie had been about sex. Now they were about something else. She knew it was love, but he was still getting there. So she'd give him time. "We're different now. It's just one more week."

Charlie met her eyes for an instant, and then turned and walked back to the booth.

Allie felt light-headed. Probably from not breathing, she decided and consciously filled her lungs with air.

She was dying from not having him, but she didn't want him yet. She wanted him more than anything.

But not yet. Not until they both knew it was more than sex.

THREE WEEKS into the bet, Allie was trying to look on the bright side and failing. It should have been easy to look on the bright side. Charlie All Night was a huge hit. The paper ran stories about Charlie and the city building, Charlie and the FoodStop indictment, Charlie and Sam. Pictures of Charlie and Sam were particularly popular, and people had donated so much dog formula and food and puppy toys to the station that they were supplying the local animal-rescue groups daily. Even the sabotage was helping; when the ad tapes disappeared from the booth one night, Charlie had been forced to fake it. His ad-libs about how great McCarthy's cashew chicken was at two o'clock in the morning, how much Sam loved the formula he'd gotten from Paula's Pet Emporium, and how Harry swore by Gleason's Auto Parts, had started a trend. Now all the advertisers wanted Charlie ad-libbing ads. He was a radio natural.

And she was going crazy. For the first time in her adult life, her first thoughts on waking weren't about the radio station. They were about Charlie. She'd gotten what she wanted: they talked all the time now. About radio, about food, about politics, about books, about sports…they talked until she was ready to scream, "Shut up and kiss me!" And even if she did, he'd probably think it was a request and play Mary Chapin Carpenter. She was delighted her career was back in high gear, but she wanted Charlie back more.

She finally hit bottom one night after staring hopelessly at Charlie through the booth window for the entire show. She was a mess and she needed comfort, so she went home and knocked on Joe's door.

"Come in," he said, half-asleep, and she went in and sat on the side of his bed while he tried to focus on her.

"I know it's the middle of the night," she said. "I'm sorry."

"No problem." He yawned and moved over and she crawled in bed next to him, sinking down on his shoulder when he put his arm around her. "So what's up?"

"You were right," she said into his shoulder.

"I'm always right." He patted her. "Let me guess. This is about Charlie."

Allie nodded. "I'm in love with him. I really screwed up this time."

"Well, not necessarily." Joe shifted in the bed to make more room for her. "This could be a good thing. At least you've given up thinking a career is a life. And everybody should fall in love at least once in her life, so that's good, too."

"I was in love with Mark," Allie said miserably. "I served my time."

Joe scowled at her. "You were not in love with Mark. Mark was your career and you thought it would be efficient to have a relationship with him, too. That was your tidy streak talking." He stared off into space for a moment. "Now, Charlie is the worst possible match for you, so this must be love. Good for you, kid."

"Very funny." Allie wanted to stick out her chin

and move away to show she wasn't kidding, but Joe's arm was too much of a comfort to lose. "What am I going to do?"

Joe shrugged. "Love him. What else can you do?"

Allie blinked, trying not to cry. "He's going to leave in November. Do you know how much that's going to hurt?"

"Do you have a choice? And anyway, it's not November yet. You've got some time. Things could change. As usual, you're focusing on the problem and not looking at the big picture."

"What big picture?" Allie slumped deeper into the bed. "There is no big picture. I love him and he's leaving in a week."

"You could leave with him, you know," Joe said, and Allie looked at him sharply. "Well, I'd miss you, but you'd write and come back to visit. It might not be a bad life, following Charlie around the country. You'd have a good time."

"And no career," Allie said stubbornly.

"It would be a choice," Joe said. "But at least it's a choice. And I think you're forgetting Charlie here, too."

Allie groaned. "Fat chance. He's all I think about anymore. I'm becoming *obsessed* with Charlie."

"Well, he's not exactly ignoring you." Allie blinked at him, and Joe went on. "I know he moved out, but that was the only sane thing he could do. He never takes his eyes off you when he's with you. He always knows exactly where you are. And..." Joe paused, and Allie waited hopefully for some killer point that would convince her falling in love with

Charlie wasn't the dumbest thing she'd ever done in her life. "He's jealous as hell of Mark."

Allie slumped again. "Big deal. I want him to love me."

Joe rolled his eyes. "Well, Al, I'm pretty sure he does."

Allie sat up, "Then why doesn't he *say* so. Why doesn't he say, 'Allie, I love you and I'm not leaving you in November.' I'm not looking for a marriage proposal here. I'm just trying to get my option extended for another year."

Joe moved his arm away. "You know, if I didn't like you and Charlie so much, I'd enjoy watching the two of you be dumb about this. Allie, he's not going to tell you he loves you until he figures it out for himself."

Allie threw her hands up in exasperation. "Well, when's that going to be?"

"Hard telling," Joe said. "I like Charlie a lot, but he's not deep, and he really hates commitment. It may take him a while."

Allie flopped back onto the pillows. "Well, great. With my luck, he'll figure it out next spring when he's in Dubuque or Broken Arrow or someplace else I'm not."

"Then you make the first move. Tell him you love him. Tell him he loves you." Joe punched his pillow and slid back down into the bed. "Produce yourself a love affair."

"He would run like a rabbit." Allie sighed. "I'm sorry. You've got to get up and work in the morning. I shouldn't have bothered you." She started to climb out of bed.

"Don't be wimpy," Joe said from his pillow. "Of course you should have bothered me. You'll be okay. Charlie will get around to figuring out what he wants as soon as he finishes doing whatever it is he came to do."

Allie turned back to him. "What do you mean?"

Joe's voice was sleepy. "Well, he came here for something. What was it?"

Allie blinked at him. "To fill in for Waldo as a favor for Bill."

Joe yawned. "Then why is he asking so many questions?"

"Because…" Allie let her voice trail off. He *was* asking a lot of questions. She'd assumed it was for the show, but he didn't care about the show. Or did he? Maybe he was getting interested in radio. He was making sure nobody was sabotaging the show again. And he had her researching great topics for the show, like this drug legalization thing they were doing next week.

"Maybe he's starting to care about the show," she told Joe with hope in her voice.

Joe snored, and she gave up and went to bed, still miserably in love but vaguely comforted.

After all, November was still a week away.

"MARK TRIED to do a talk show with Lisa today," Harry told Charlie. "You've really got to start getting up earlier. You're missing some good stuff."

Charlie sat on the console. "Such as?"

"He decided they were going to discuss working relationships."

"Well, it's an okay topic," Charlie said.

"Yeah." Harry leaned back. "But Mark spent the

whole time talking about Allie. Never let Lisa get a word in edgewise. She finally burst into tears and left the booth.''

"We need to kick him,'' Charlie said. "I don't care how dumb he is, that was mean.''

"Nah,'' Harry said. "He still doesn't know why she's upset. And she's staying with him. They deserve each other.'' He tilted the chair back to look up at Charlie. "I think he's planning on making his move on Allie again.''

Charlie ignored the spurt of alarm he felt and shrugged. "She can take care of herself.''

Harry shook his head. "Yeah, but you're not around to stick up for your interests much. You don't even see her outside of work.''

"Come on,'' Charlie protested. "I see her five or six hours a day.''

"At work,'' Harry said. "It sort of looks like, if you're not sleeping with her, why spend time with her?''

"Hey,'' Charlie said. "That's not—''

"That's what it looks like. And Mark has noticed. Probably mentioned it to Allie by now, too.''

Allie came into the booth. "Here's the stuff you wanted,'' she told Charlie, handing him a stack of notes. "I got the—''

"You busy tomorrow night?'' Charlie asked her.

"Uh, no.'' She blinked up at him.

"Let's get a video and some Chinese,'' he said. "Tell Joe.''

"Joe's got a date. It'd be just us.''

"Oh.'' Charlie shrugged. "Okay. Fine.''

"Okay." Allie looked at him strangely again and left the booth.

"Good move," Harry told him.

"Right," Charlie said, but he thought, *Allie and me and Chinese food at her apartment. Oh, hell.*

HARRY CAME OUT of the booth, and Allie looked at him with suspicion. "What are you up to?"

"Me? Nothing." Harry grinned at her. "Have a good time tomorrow night."

"Did you put him up to that?"

"Nope. Thought of it on his own. 'Bout time, too, don't you think?"

Allie narrowed her eyes at him. "Harry, you wouldn't lie to me, would you?"

"Nope." Harry went off down the hall whistling.

Well, he was up to something. But she was going to see Charlie, outside the radio station, for an entire evening, so it really didn't matter.

For the first time in a long while, she began to look forward to the next day.

"YOU KNOW, Mark's up to something," Allie told Charlie during the news break.

"Oh, there's a surprise," Charlie said. "Of course he's up to something. He wants you back."

Allie blinked. "I don't think so. But I do think he's trying to ruin your show. I think he's the one—"

"Our show," Charlie corrected her. "It's our show. I know he's trying to ruin it. I found our missing promo tapes in his office. But he's also trying to get you back. I may have to hit him, after all."

"Why?" Allie looked at him in exasperation. "You're leaving next week. Why should you care?"

"Because I'd hate to think any woman could go from me to Mark," he said.

"Well, since you won't be here to watch, I don't see what difference it makes." Allie turned away from him in disgust. "You think I'm going to give up men just because you're leaving?"

Charlie watched through the booth windows as she stomped away. *Yeah,* he thought. *That's exactly what I want.* Then he picked up the headset and waited for the news to end while he mentally kicked himself for ever coming to Tuttle in the first place.

SATURDAY NIGHT, Charlie brought her *American Dreamer* because she'd said that was her favorite movie, and sat with her on the couch and laughed and felt better than he had since he'd moved out.

"I miss this." Charlie took her hand when the movie was over. "I miss watching videos and arguing with you over the Chinese food and waking up with you. I miss the physical stuff, too, but I miss this the most."

"I know." Allie tightened her hand on his, and he paid attention to the warmth of her grip and the softness of her skin pressed against his. "I want you here so I can tell you things, and so you can listen to Joe's jokes."

"Joe's jokes are the worst." Charlie grinned at her and watched her smile in response, watched the light in her eyes, and the way her cheeks bloomed with the smile, and the way her head tilted, just a little, toward him. "I miss Joe's jokes a lot."

"Mostly, I just miss having you here." She brushed her cheek against his shoulder, and he closed his eyes with pleasure. "You don't even have to watch the movie or listen to Joe's jokes. Just be here."

He opened his eyes then, and she was so right, so everything he wanted forever, and he wanted to say, "I love you, Allie," but it wasn't fair. He was leaving in a week. It wasn't fair.

It was true, but it wasn't fair.

Maybe Allie would like traveling. Maybe Allie would love him enough to leave with him in November.

"What's wrong?" she asked softly and he bent to hear her, and that brought him to her mouth and he kissed her, moving his lips gently against hers, feeling the surge in his throat and chest and groin, but feeling the swell in his heart more. Her hand came up to his cheek, and when the kiss was done she let her lips travel there and then kissed his eyelids and then his lips again, and he ached with love for her. "Why is it," he whispered against her cheek, "that we didn't start making love until we stopped sleeping together?"

She shook her head wordlessly and settled into his arms, and he held her and memorized the weight and the feel of her, and the scent of her hair, and soft rhythm of her heart against his, and he felt something break away inside him, the tension and the guardedness and everything that had kept him away from her.

A few minutes later, for the first time in almost three weeks, he fell dreamlessly asleep.

ON MONDAY, the *Tuttle Tribune* began a series on the history of the city building, killing forever any hopes the mayor might have had of building a new one, and making Charlie a household word once again.

"That's our boy," Joe said when he saw the first article, and Allie, remembering a warm, if platonic, weekend, said, "We can only hope."

Later that afternoon, Lisa came to see her. "It's awful, Allie," Lisa moaned to her in her office. "I can't do anything right. I hate it. No matter what I do, Mark thinks it isn't enough or it isn't done right or *something.*"

"So quit." Allie stacked the notes she'd gathered for the drug legalization show and put them in a folder for Charlie who would actually read them on his own instead of insisting she explain them to him the way Mark had. Thank God, she wasn't stuck with Mark anymore. She felt positively sympathetic toward Lisa. "Leave him. You don't have to take that."

"But it's the *drive-time show,*" Lisa wailed, and Allie was about to say, "So what?" when she remembered why that was important. At least, it had been important to her a month before. And if Lisa quit, Mark would offer her the producing spot again. He'd made that very clear. In fact, knowing Mark as she did, Allie had a sneaking suspicion he might be forcing Lisa to quit. Then Bill would ask her to step in to save the prime-time show.

She shook her head at the thought. Not in a million years. The hell with drive time. She was doing better in the middle of the night with the weirdos and Charlie, a redundant thought if there ever was one.

"The drive-time show isn't everything," she said to Lisa. "If you're this unhappy, leave. Ask Marcia to take you. She's not happy with her producer."

"And lose the drive-time show?" Lisa stood up. "Oh, no. I'm sticking it out." Lisa stomped out of the office, and Allie let her go. She had enough problems without counseling career-obsessed radio producers.

She had Charlie.

"YOU KNOW, I've been thinking," Harry said Tuesday afternoon in front of the TV. "You're still leaving in November, right?"

"Right," Charlie said with a lot more conviction than he felt.

"Well, then, I'm gonna make my move on Allie."

Charlie spilled his beer. "What?"

Harry held up his hand. "Not until you're gone, of course. Wouldn't dream of it. But once you're out of the picture…well, wouldn't you rather she was with me than with Mark?"

Charlie scowled at him. "That's Allie's business."

Harry nodded. "Exactly. So I thought I'd ask her to produce my show and then just see what developed. It's time I started thinking about getting married again. I've been thinking about it and you're right. I don't think Sheila's coming back."

Charlie took a deep breath. "Well, you never know—"

"Nope." Harry shook his head. "You were right. It's time I moved on with my life, got a contingency plan. I'd have never thought of it if it wasn't for you." He gave Charlie a serious nod. "Thanks, buddy."

"No problem," Charlie snarled and got up to get another beer, wondering why the hell he hadn't kept his mouth shut.

Back in the living room, Harry grinned and finished his beer.

WEDNESDAY MORNING, Allie met Joe in the kitchen for breakfast, stopping in her tracks when she saw the look on his face.

"This is bad," he said, and handed her the paper.

"Local DJ Former Drug Dealer," the headline flared at her. "Charlie 'Ten' Tenniel arrested for drug trafficking in Lawrenceville, disappears for months before arriving in Tuttle as the WBBB wonder boy. Do we want this element in our town?"

Allie looked up at Joe and shook her head. "No. Charlie did not deal drugs. He lived with us. He doesn't even smoke. His limit is two beers. He's not a druggie."

Joe sat down. "Look, they've screwed up before, but this time they have what looks like evidence. It was in the Lawrenceville paper. They have quotes from Lawrenceville reporters. There's some truth somewhere."

"Charlie doesn't do drugs," Allie said firmly. "I don't care what the paper says."

"All right." Joe sat back. "I've got to admit, that's my gut reaction, too. But…"

Allie met his eyes. "But nothing. He's innocent."

"But I wish you weren't so involved with him," Joe finished. "I don't want you hurt. You're unhappy enough because he's leaving. I don't want you to feel cheated, too."

"He's innocent." Allie frowned. "I know he's innocent."

CHARLIE MET HER in her office that afternoon. "I suppose you've seen the paper," he said, and she knew he was watching for her reaction.

"It's not you." She lifted her chin. "I don't know what's going on, but it's not you."

He leaned in the doorway. "There's a lot of evidence in that article, Allie. How can you be sure?"

"I know you." She snapped it out with more force than she'd meant to. "You're not that way. You wouldn't do that."

Charlie closed his eyes. "I do not deserve you, but I'm damn grateful just the same."

"Sure you deserve me," Allie said. "Anything you want to tell me before I start calling everybody I know in journalism to track this down?"

"No," Charlie said. "Don't call anyone. Just let this be."

Allie gawked at him. "Are you nuts? We have to stop this. We have to—"

"No," Charlie said. "I don't want it stopped."

Allie swallowed and tried again. "Charlie, this will be murder on the show. Drugs are not classy in Tuttle. This will kill us."

He winced. "I hadn't thought of that. I'm sorry, Al, I really am, but don't stop the story. Don't track it down. Let it play. It's important to me."

"Why?" The flatness of the question broke the mood they'd shared.

"You'll have to trust me on this," he told her, and her temper broke.

"I have to trust you that you're not a dealer, and I do," she said to him. "But you can't trust me with the truth."

"It's not my secret," Charlie said, and the only thing that kept her from screaming at him was how miserable he looked. "I'll tell you as soon as it's over, but it's not my secret."

"So I'm supposed to just sit here and let that damn article ruin us both while you keep somebody else's secret." Allie started to shake with rage and frustration. "What the hell is going on here?"

Charlie rubbed his hand over the back of his head. "Don't worry about it. This will be over soon. You'll be fine, I swear."

"Right," she snapped. "I'll be fine because I'll be breaking in a new guy in a week, and you'll be fine because you're leaving this mess behind you, right? We'll all be fine. Great."

"Allie," Charlie began, and she cut him off.

"Go away. Just go away. I don't want to talk about this anymore. Just leave."

"Allie, this is important." She ignored him, but he went on, anyway. "I want us to do the show about legalizing drugs tonight. I want you to be against it so I can argue for it."

She gaped at him. "Have you lost your mind? After this article…" Her voice trailed off. "You want people to think this is true." She sat back in her chair. "*Why?*"

"Just for a little while," he told her. "I'm almost there. This article could do it for me."

"Almost *where?*" Allie's annoyance blanked everything out. "You can't possibly think I'm going to help you ruin this show and my own reputation without some explanation here. Either tell me what's going on, or you're on your own tonight."

Charlie started to say something, and then he sighed, and said, ''All right, that's fair, I'll do it myself,'' and left the office.

Allie put her head down on the desk. The show was ruined, Charlie didn't trust her, and he was still leaving in November.

And she couldn't think of a damn thing to do about any of it except go home and cry in Joe's arms.

THE NEXT MONDAY—after three polite work nights and one miserably lonely weekend, after the calls to the show had dropped off to hecklers who wanted to score off Charlie's arrest record and outraged citizens who wanted him off the air; after Charlie had disappeared for long stretches of time and the police had dropped by to see him—things hit bottom.

Charlie's wife showed up.

She was a little thing, dark and sort of wet with tears, and she was about seven or eight months' pregnant. Karen called Allie to the desk and pointed to her and said, ''You're not going to like this. She's looking for Ten Tenniel. She says she's married to him.''

Not possible, Allie told herself, but the list of possibilities for Charlie had been growing since he'd refused to defend himself on the drug charge. She still believed in him, but it was harder.

She went toward the girl. ''Hello, I'm Alice Mc-Guffey, Mr. Tenniel's producer and—''

''Where is he?'' The girl stood up and looked at her defiantly. ''He's my husband, and I want to see him.''

''He's not here right now, but he should be in any time,'' Allie said. ''Would you like to wait in my office?'' She looked around to see Stewart and Lisa listening in from the hallway. ''It's more private there.''

''Where is he?'' the girl demanded again, and then with his usual impeccable timing, Charlie came through the doors and stopped when he saw her. ''Miranda?''

''Charlie?'' She seemed as amazed as he was.

''Don't say anything,'' Charlie told her, taking her arm. ''We can talk out here.''

''Charlie?'' Allie said, outraged.

Charlie shoved Miranda out into the hall and pointed at Allie. ''You stay here and stop thinking dumb thoughts. You know me better than this. I'll be back as soon as I can.''

''Wait a minute!'' Allie said, incensed, but he was shoving Miranda into an elevator by then and she was left with her own murderous thoughts and Karen and Stewart and Lisa staring at her with sympathy and avid curiosity.

This time she was going to kill him.

But first she was going to find out what the hell was going on.

HE CAME INTO her office half an hour before the show and caught her dialing the phone.

''I know.'' He held up his hand to stop her from talking. ''I'm a creep for leaving you like that. I had to call my dad and put Miranda on a bus home before I could explain. I know you're mad at me and I deserve it, but just let me explain.''

''Oh, *now* you're going to explain.'' Allie slapped the phone down. ''Well, that's just great.''

''Allie, I'm not—''

"Ten Tenniel. I know. She's your brother's wife, right?"

Charlie sat down. "Well, sort of. They're not actually married. How did you figure it out?"

Allie shook her head, disgusted with him. "It wasn't hard once I woke up. You wouldn't let us call you Ten and that's what the Lawrenceville station was famous for. And you may be a natural on radio, but Harry was right. You didn't have any idea what you were doing that first night. So you came here pretending to be your brother, and since Bill knows your family, he knows that, too. So whatever secret you're keeping is Bill's, and this whole program thing was just a blind, and I've been killing myself to make you a success for nothing."

"Well, I told you not to do it," Charlie pointed out mildly. "Which part are you the most mad about?"

"That you didn't trust me," Allie said, her anger evaporating from the hurt. "You didn't trust me at all."

"It wasn't that." Charlie put his head in his hands. "I don't know how the hell this got so complicated. I trusted you. I knew it wasn't you from the beginning. But you go charging in on everything you do, and that was the wrong way to do this."

Allie leaned forward. "To do what? What do you mean it wasn't me?"

Charlie met her eyes. "Somebody's running drugs from the station. Bill got an anonymous letter and used it as an excuse to get me down here as a favor to my dad. He wanted to know about the letter because he thought it was a smear, and my dad wanted me to get a real job, so they cooked it up between them. And I bought it, and I've been trying to find a link between the mayor or Roger Preston or Mark and drugs. Nothing. So for the past week I've been letting the drug story slide, running around pretending to be a dealer, trying to figure things out. And last night, going over your drug legalization notes, I finally did.''

"Who is it?" Allie asked when she found her voice. "I can't believe it. Who's dealing?"

"Grady," Charlie said. "It has to be Grady."

Nine

"Are you out of your mind?" Allie looked at him in horror. "Grady is the last person to push drugs. He doesn't care about money. He—"

"He cares about his mother," Charlie said. "And Mrs. Winthrop and Mrs. Wexman and all the rest."

Allie shook her head. "I don't get it."

"I didn't get it either at first." Charlie looked so miserable she wanted to go to him, but not until he stopped saying stupid things about Grady. "Grady grows it behind his dome, but that wasn't enough because I knew Grady wouldn't deal drugs for money. But the fraternity kids said we were giving it away, and then I read your notes on drug legalization and the stuff you found on cancer patients. That's when it all fell into place."

Allie closed her eyes. "I remember. Pot helps people handle chemo." Then she had a thought and her eyes flew open again. "Grady gave Beattie pot?"

Charlie nodded. "He'd do anything to help her. And if Beattie knew it helped her, she'd insist on sharing it with others. They've been providing pot for the town's cancer patients. That's why Mrs. Winthrop's grandson got nasty with her. He wanted her stash."

"Oh, God." Allie put her head in her hands. "And

that's why people bring Grady cookies and things. They're trying to say thank you." She tilted her head back and thought for a moment. "Well, okay. Now we know. All we have to do is keep out mouths shut about it—"

"No," Charlie said. "We can't. This is illegal."

Allie gaped at him. "You can't possibly be thinking of turning Grady in?"

He sighed. "You're not listening. I'm going to tell Grady I know, and he's going to turn himself in. It's illegal, Al. And he's running out of time. That little Winthrop brat sent the letter to Bill. Everybody at the college knows somebody here is dealing. And I've been asking questions. There was that newspaper piece about me being a pusher that made the police start watching me. They know who I've been talking to, and they know something's up. There's going to be hell to pay, and if Grady turns himself in, he's at least got that in his favor. It's too late for anything else."

"No." Allie came around the desk and headed for the door. "No. We can stop this. We can stonewall this. Grady is not going to jail."

Charlie caught her arm. "Don't say anything to anybody. Let me handle this."

"Like you've handled it so far?" Allie looked up at him, furious. "If you hadn't poked around, we'd be fine. Who is he hurting? He's helping people, and you're going to turn him in." Allie yanked her arm away from him. "This is the worst. You're just going to stand there and watch him go to prison."

"What do you want me to do?" Charlie said.

"You started this mess," she said. "You should fix it."

"I can't fix it. All I can do is see it through to the end."

Allie looked at him, uncomprehending. "I can't believe you're doing this. You're not even going to try to work something else out. You're just going to go ahead and do it your way."

"Allie—"

"Just like Bill," she said to him, knowing it would hurt him. "Just like your dad."

His mouth tightened, and then he left the office.

"Boy, I sure can pick them," she said to nobody in particular, and then devoted all her energy to not crying.

Mark stuck his head in the door. "Say, I just heard about Charlie's wife. That's a really bad break, Allie. Let me take you out to dinner." He smiled at her, looking as gorgeous as ever, and she wanted him dead, too.

"Get out of here," she snarled.

"Maybe tomorrow," he said and escaped out the door.

Allie went back to her chair and thought about tomorrow. She had to think of a plan. Soon.

CHARLIE WAITED until Grady came into the booth during the news at quarter to two before he said anything to him.

"You look like hell," Grady said when he saw him. "Take off, I'll take it from here."

"I can't." Charlie looked at him miserably. "I hate this. You have no idea how much I hate this."

Grady blinked at him. "What's wrong?"

Charlie sighed. "I know you give pot to cancer patients. In fact, a hell of a lot of Tuttle knows you give pot away, Grady. It's all over.''

Grady pushed Sam's basket to one side and sat down on the counter. "Oh.'' Sam poked his head out, and Grady scratched him behind his ears. "Well, that depends. Are you going to turn me in?''

Charlie shook his head. "No, you're going to turn yourself in. That should work in your favor. With your dad's lawyers—''

"My dad will disown me,'' Grady said, but he didn't seem too upset at the thought. "What can I do to convince you this isn't the best way to do this?''

"Anything,'' Charlie said fervently. "You have no idea how much I want to be convinced. But this is going to blow any minute, Grady. Too many people know. You're a lot better off doing this yourself than waiting until they come for you.''

Grady sat looking lost in thought for a moment. Then he met Charlie's eyes. "Can I have some time?''

"All you want,'' Charlie said. "But don't take too long. You'll lose the only advantage you have.''

"How did you find out?'' Grady asked him as he got up to go.

"The rumors. Your crop out in back. The chemo. The cookies and stuff. It finally all came together.'' Charlie shook his head. "I'm really sorry, Grady. I know you were doing it for a good reason.''

"Which is why I don't want to stop.'' Grady sat down in the chair. "Let me think about this and I'll talk to you tomorrow.''

"Great,'' Charlie said. "Something else to look forward to.''

THE NEXT MORNING, Allie still hadn't thought of a plan even after talking the whole mess over with Joe.

"There's a mandatory prison sentence for possession," he told her. "And Bill isn't going to be much help once he finds out Grady's been getting his mother stoned."

"That's a stupid law," Allie said. "The stuff is medicinal, for heaven's sake."

Then Joe opened the paper, said, "Oh, hell," and handed it to her.

There was a picture of Charlie putting Miranda on the bus, captioned Local DJ Abandons Pregnant Wife. Allie stared at it grimly. She was furious with Charlie, but he didn't deserve this.

Then she had a new thought. How had the photographer known to be at the bus station? Somebody had tipped off the paper. Somebody at WBBB.

This one they couldn't blame on the mayor. She got dressed and went into the station early.

Allie was standing outside the booth when Mark came out at ten.

"Allie!" He all but ran over Lisa to get to her. "What a great surprise!"

"I decided to take you up on that lunch offer," Allie told him. "You free now?"

"We have a conference after every show," Lisa put in. "Sometimes they last a long time."

"Not today." Mark took Allie's arm. "We'll skip it today."

"But Mark," Lisa said.

"Forget it." Mark steered Allie toward the lobby. "This is just great. I've got a lot I want to tell you."

"Good," Allie said. "There's a lot I want to hear."

"IT JUST HASN'T BEEN the same without you," Mark began when they were seated at the Settle Inn. "I've been—"

"You've been busy," Allie said. "That was you who played all those tricks on Charlie, wiping the tapes, stealing his promos, making the prank calls."

"Well..." Mark seemed at a loss. "I may have gone too far, but it was all—"

"And then you gave the story about Charlie's wife to the paper. That was a good one." Allie tried to keep her voice noncommittal.

He looked at her warily. "I might have mentioned it."

"Why?"

"Well, Lisa called me and told me about it, and I thought that the people of Tuttle should know what kind of guy he is." Mark shifted in his chair. "You know, leaving his wife pregnant and all. I thought you should know, too. He's not the kind of guy for you, Allie."

Allie fought down the urge to reach across the table and strangle him. "Oh? And what kind of guy is?"

Mark took a deep breath. "Well, me." He held up his hand to stop her protest. "I know I made a mistake when I broke up with you, but believe me, I know it now. I was stupid. You want me to come crawling back, I will. Whatever you say."

Allie shook her head at him in disgusted amazement. "And what about Lisa? She's been working her butt off for you."

"Lisa's a child." Mark settled back in his chair. "A lovely child, but still a child. The experience I've given her will look good on her résumé—"

"Oh, you want me back as a *producer*." Allie nodded. "I misunderstood."

"No, no! I want you back completely." Mark leaned forward. "I think we should get married."

"Married." Allie nodded. "Married. You're going to go back across the street and tell Lisa that you're dumping her as your producer and your girlfriend to marry me."

"Absolutely." Mark beamed at her. "I'm a big enough man to admit my mistakes."

"You're a dweeb." Allie stood up. "If you do anything else to sabotage Charlie's show, I will tell Bill and insist that he fire you. I mean it. Stay away from Charlie. And while you're at it, stay away from me."

"Allie!" Mark stood up to follow her.

"No." Allie put out her hand to stop him. "I can't believe you pulled this stuff just to save your career. What did you think you were doing?"

Mark blinked at her. "What you taught me to do. Make the show the best."

"I never taught you to sabotage other shows to do it," Allie said, appalled, but she knew he was right. The entire time she'd been with him, the show had been everything. She'd just forgotten to teach him morals before she'd left. "There's more to life than radio, Mark."

"Not to my life," he said, and she felt sorry for him because he was right again.

"Go make up with Lisa," she told him. "You're going to need her."

"Harry told me you had lunch with Mark today," Charlie said when she walked into the booth at ten.

"Harry told you right." Allie handed him the notes and the promos.

"Have a good time?"

"He asked me to marry him." Allie turned and walked out of the booth to the production table.

"He *what?*" Charlie snapped over the headset.

"He offered me the producing slot, too," Allie said through her mike. "The news is almost over. Stand by."

"Screw the news," Charlie said. "Did you say yes?"

Allie glared at him. "What possible difference could it make to you since you're leaving tomorrow?"

"None," Charlie said. "Did you say yes?"

"No," Allie said. "I said no."

"Could we stop fighting and talk about this?" Charlie asked her once his heart was out of his throat.

"Why?" Allie looked at him miserably. "Nothing's changed. I told him to stop sabotaging your show, but I don't know why I bothered. You're leaving tomorrow. You're turning Grady in. It's all over, anyway."

Charlie looked at her just as miserably and said, "All right. Whatever you want." The news went off and he moved up the mike slide and said, "Good evening, Tuttle. You're with Charlie All Night—"

Allie took off her headphones. He could do the broadcast without her by now. It wasn't as if it mattered. It was his last show. He was going to be gone in another twenty-four hours and then she could put her life back together without him.

She could hardly wait.

THEY DID THE REST of the show with silence between them, Charlie just playing music. The worst was when he did a Paul Anka double play for Sam—"Puppy Love" and "Put Your Head On My Shoulder"—and patted the puppy on his own shoulder until Sam gave up and went to sleep. She loved him so much then, she hurt with it. He only stopped to talk once, this time about the use of marijuana in treating the nausea associated with chemotherapy. He made a good persuasive argument, and Allie knew he was doing it for Grady's sake, to prepare the way for Grady's defense, but it wasn't enough.

He was still going to turn Grady in.

She stayed until Grady showed up at quarter to two to take over the booth.

"Grady, I'm sorry," she told him when he came in. "If there's anything I can do…"

Grady shook his head. "Nope. I got myself into this. I'm ready."

"Oh, Grady," Allie said, but he'd already gone into the booth with Charlie.

Charlie plugged the news cassette in and she watched them as he gave Grady the chair and then leaned on the side of the booth to talk to him. Charlie looked like death, exhaustion and unhappiness making him haggard. For a moment, she relented because she loved him.

Then she went in to try one last time to convince him.

"You can't do this," she said when she was in the booth with them. "I've tried and tried to think of a way around this, but I can't. Joe says a prison sentence is mandatory. You can't do this."

Charlie closed his eyes against her. "It's the law. I

know Grady did what he did because he loves his mother—''

"He saved her life," Allie broke in. "She couldn't eat. He saved—"

"But the law is the law," Charlie went on inexorably. "He broke it."

Allie looked at Grady for help. "I don't believe this. The law is stupid. In fact, the law is *wrong*—"

"Listen to me," Charlie said and the intensity in his voice stopped her in midsentence. "One of the biggest problems this country has is that people think a law is only a law if they agree with it. And if they don't, it's all right to kick guys like Joe out of the service and bomb abortion clinics because there's a *higher law* at work. And that's garbage, Allie. The law is the law. If you don't like it, change it. But don't break it and then start whining when there are consequences."

"But they won't change it," Allie snapped. "Politicians are such cowards when it comes to legalizing any drugs that they'd rather see people die than risk their careers. It's not going to change. And it's *wrong*."

"The law is the law," Charlie said. "You can't choose which part of it you like and which you're going to ignore. It's not a salad bar, Al. The whole thing stands, or the whole thing goes. And Grady broke the law."

"And you're going to turn him in." Allie stood there, her eyes blazing at him in contempt. "Good old by-the-book, my-way-is-law Charlie. I bet you look a whole lot like your father now."

Charlie winced, and Grady stood up and said,

"Wait a minute." His voice was low and mild but it cut through her anger. "Thanks for the defense, Al. I appreciate it. But Charlie's right. Don't do the crime if you can't do the time." He turned to Charlie. "I'm only asking one favor."

Charlie nodded.

"Don't turn me in until tomorrow morning. Let me finish the show and tell my mom and dad first."

Charlie knew he was right, and he'd never felt worse in his life, knowing he was ruining Grady's life, knowing Allie would probably never speak to him again. It was a lot to pay for being right. "Of course I won't," he told Grady.

Grady looked him in the eye. "I won't run."

Charlie swallowed. "I know that. Oh, hell, Grady." He cast around for something to say.

Grady sat back down in the console chair. "It's not your problem anymore," he told Charlie as he picked up the headphones. "In fact, if I hadn't started doing this, you wouldn't have been here at all. So it's always been my problem. Sorry I dragged you into it."

"I'm sorry you did, too," Allie said.

Charlie looked at her. "I'm not sorry. I wouldn't trade these past weeks for anything."

"Well, I would," she said, and there were tears in her voice. "I'd trade them for Grady's freedom. You're going to send him to prison. Do you know how long he'll be there? Do you know how awful—"

"Allie, let it go," Grady said. "I'm not a kid. Stop treating me like one. This isn't Charlie's fault."

"Well, it sure looks that way to me," Allie said and walked out of the booth, and Charlie felt all the warmth and air leave the room with her.

He was right. He knew he was right.

But being right without Allie was lousy. And that was going to be the story for the rest of his life.

Grady rubbed his forehead. "She'll calm down. She'll see there was nothing else you could do."

"Will she?" Charlie sat on the edge of the console. "*I'm* not even sure there was nothing else I could do. You're not a criminal."

"Well, yeah, I am," Grady said. "I committed a crime. I'm pretty sure that makes me a criminal."

"And she was right about something else." Charlie looked unhappily at Grady. "I'm acting just like my father. And yours. Rigid."

Grady shook his head. "My dad told me about your brother. Your father covered up your brother's crime. You're doing the opposite. You're on the side of the angels."

"Pretty lousy angels." Charlie tipped his head back. "I know I'm right. My dad knew he was right. Bill always knows he's right. I'm everything I never wanted to be. I've spent my whole life refusing to have anything to do with people so that I'd never try to control anybody. And now I'm alone and still controlling people. What I should do is just leave town now. I know you'll tell Bill, so my job's done." He felt so tired his bones ached. "I should just go now."

"And leave everybody?" Grady looked incredulous. "Not say goodbye to Harry or Joe or Karen? Or Allie?"

Charlie laughed shortly. "I don't think Allie will talk to me long enough to let me say goodbye."

Grady watched him for a moment and then shrugged. "Then go. I'll tell them all you said so-long.'' He straightened as the music stopped and leaned in to the mike to begin his show intro, and Charlie backed out of the booth as soundlessly as possible. He listened to Grady for a few minutes, talking about herbal teas this time, and then he picked up his coat and left.

ALLIE DROVE around for a while, trying to make sense of what had happened. Charlie's arguments sounded right, but there were Grady and Beattie and Mrs. Winthrop, and they weren't wrong. So how could Charlie be right? There should have been a simple answer, and there wasn't.

She stopped and picked up cashew chicken and pot stickers because she was unhappy and starving and because it was what she wanted, for some reason.

Then she went home, and turned on Grady's show, and thought about the mess some more.

She wanted to hate Charlie for what he was going to do to Grady, but she didn't. She loved him. And tomorrow was November and he was leaving, and she'd be alone again, picking up the pieces he'd left behind him.

Well, not alone. She had Joe. And Harry. And Karen and Marcia, and even Mark and Lisa weren't a complete loss. And Bill and Beattie and most of all Grady. She'd be working her butt off for Grady because he deserved it. She'd find a way to keep him out of jail.

And she'd get the drive-time show back. Mark would take her back in a heartbeat: the last thing he needed was her making some new bozo the flavor of the month the way she'd done with Charlie. He still didn't get it that she hadn't done it alone. That they'd been a team.

Allie closed her eyes for a moment because it hurt so much to remember that. In the background, Grady was playing some weird chanting music. Who would play the weird stuff while Grady was in prison?

The doorbell rang, and Allie went to get it, assuming Joe had forgotten his key and grateful he was home to comfort her.

But when she opened the door, Charlie said, "Can we please talk about this?"

Allie stood silent, staring at him as he filled her doorway. She blinked back tears and tried to breathe. The worst thing she could do would be to cry all over him; he was her problem, not her solution. But he stood there, tall and broad and solid and safe, and he sure looked like all her solutions for the rest of her life.

And tomorrow was November and Grady was going to jail.

He came in and closed the door and took her hand and pulled her over to the couch. Then he sat down beside her, and she held herself rigid so she wouldn't lean into him, trying not to collapse against him, furious with him for what he was doing to Grady, loving him so much she was paralyzed with it.

"I don't want to leave it like this," Charlie said. "This is not the way we do things. Scream at me or something, but don't walk away from me."

Allie swallowed, and her voice came out strained. "I don't know what to scream. I know you're right. And I know you're wrong. And I'm so tired, and you're leaving anyway." She tipped her head back and stared at the cracks in the ceiling. One of the cracks curved around itself and looked vaguely like Australia so she concentrated on that. All her other thoughts hurt too much.

"My father got my brother off the hook on his drug charge," Charlie said. "Bought off the witnesses and slung Ten's butt into a rehab center. He got Ten so buried, he couldn't even call his girlfriend. But he solved the problem. My mother was not embarrassed. My brother was not jailed. And the law, well, the law is for the little people."

Allie turned at the pain in his voice. "Charlie, you don't have to—"

"Yeah, I do."

She could see how seriously he was looking at her, and she was too tired to argue. "All right. Tell me."

"He fixes everything the way he wants it." Charlie said. "He wanted Ten to be a success and he was. Only Ten had to deal drugs to get it. And he wanted me to settle down, so he sent me here. Bill didn't give a damn about that letter. He was doing my dad a favor, give his son a job, make him settle down. That's what my dad told Bill. I know it."

"Well, he didn't get what he wanted there," Allie said. "You're leaving tomorrow. You—"

"And I'm doing the same thing," Charlie went on. "I did what I was sent to do, fix Bill's little anony-mous-letter problem." He looked at Allie. "I know I'm right on this. But it feels wrong. It feels like my father. It feels lousy."

"You're not your father." Allie's voice was firm. "You refuse to take any responsibility for anything. You never tell anybody what to do."

"Why does that sound so bad?" Charlie slumped back against the couch. "I thought it was a solution, but it's as bad as the problem." He shook his head. "I packed my car tonight. I figured my job was done, and I hated what was happening so I thought I'd just leave. Let you play opera until you found another schmuck to make into a star."

Allie latched on to his mistake. "I didn't make you a star. You did. Your personality and your brains and your talent."

"We did." He looked at her then. "We did it together."

Allie closed her eyes because it hurt too much to look at him. "Don't. It's over. You're leaving."

"No, I'm not," he told her. "I can't. I can't leave you. I love you. I can leave Tuttle, but I can't leave you. I don't ever want to spend another day without you." He leaned toward her, and his voice was taut. "I was going to leave this whole mess behind. I got in the car to go, and then I just sat there and thought, 'Where the hell am I going?' Because without you, there isn't anyplace else to go. You're all there is."

All the air had been sucked out of her lungs. Allie felt pain in her chest and heat behind her eyelids where tears pressed, and she couldn't move from all the emotion that was choking her.

When she didn't say anything, Charlie added, "Say something, please. I'm dying here."

She tried to suck some air into her lungs. She was having trouble breathing. And speaking. "I..." The words died.

Charlie took her hand. "I love you, Al. It's not about sex or the bet or the show. I love you. I don't know, with what I've done, if that's enough, but I do love you.''

"It's enough," she said, and her voice broke. "It's enough." She swallowed. "I'm really mad at you, and I hate what you're doing to Grady…''

"I know.''

"But I love you," she said, and as she said it, any doubts she had disappeared forever. "I love you so much sometimes I get dizzy when I look at you. I feel good when I'm with you. I feel right. I think you're wrong here, but I don't think I could stand life without you.''

He bent to kiss her, and she held her breath and felt his lips on hers, warm and gentle and everything he was, and she kissed him then, with all the love she had for him, memorizing him, breathing with him as his mouth grew hot on hers.

"Don't ever leave me," he said against her lips, and she almost laughed because she wasn't the one with the need to leave, but then the chanting on the radio stopped and Grady's voice broke in.

"This will be my last show for a while, Tuttle," he said, and they both turned to listen to him, their heads close. "I've been breaking the law, and tomorrow morning, I'm turning myself in. I had a long talk with a friend tonight, and he pointed out that the law is a fine thing, even when it's wrong. It's the only defense we have against anarchy, against the strong overwhelming the weak. And if it's wrong, well, then it's our job to change it. I've been giving away marijuana to chemotherapy patients because it helps them withstand the nausea the treatments cause, but it's against the law. I think it's time this law was changed, and tonight's the only night I have left to talk about it before I go to jail. If you're listening and you have an opinion, call in. The number is—''

''Grady is the only person I know who could make his arrest a call-in topic,'' Allie said when she'd recovered her voice. ''What do you suppose he's been doing for the past hour while all that music played?''

Charlie let go of her. ''He's been talking to his father. I called Bill and told him.''

Allie sat up. ''You *what?*''

Charlie sighed. ''I called Bill and told him that Grady was doing something important that had probably saved Beattie's life, and that now it was Bill's turn to stick his neck out. He yelled a lot, but I think he saw the light at the end. I think he's going to fight for Grady. When I hung up, he was making a plan. If nothing else, it should be interesting to see what happens next.'' He picked up the chicken carton from the table in front of them and began to eat, and when Allie stole a look at him, he looked almost relaxed.

All right. It wouldn't have been her way of handling it, but at least he was handling it. Getting involved. And he might just be right. ''I bet Bill's not the only one making a plan,'' she told him, picking up the pot stickers. ''I bet Beattie's working on a beaut.''

''You should have gotten more food,'' Charlie said. ''This chicken is going to be gone in no time.''

They sat close on the couch and finished the chicken and the pot stickers while they listened to Grady and his callers, all of whom seemed ready to march on city hall to spring him if necessary. Of course, they were all Grady's callers, and anyone who would listen to Grady at three in the morning was already fanatically loyal, but it did reassure Allie. Even more reassuring was having Charlie near. She finally fell asleep on Charlie's shoulder while he listened to Grady's show, and she didn't wake up until he shook her at five-thirty.

"Come on," he told her softly. "Let's go back in and see if Grady needs help after the show."

Ten

The station was crowded when they got there at five forty-five. The lobby teemed with two TV crews, print journalists, the sheriff, a grim Bill and Beattie and a bemused Mark.

"What is this?" Mark caught Allie's arm as she came through the door behind Charlie. Charlie looked back and rolled his eyes at Mark, but he kept on going into the station hallway. "What's all the publicity for?" Mark asked. "What did Charlie do now?"

"Nothing." Allie pulled her arm away. "Grady confessed to giving away marijuana to cancer patients. He's going to be arrested."

Mark got a faraway look in his eye. Probably planning on confessing to possession of oregano. How anyone could get that caught up in a career—

She stopped. Thank God for Charlie. If it hadn't been for him, she'd still be with Mark. In fact, she'd probably *be* Mark.

"I've got to go," she told Mark and went into the station to find Charlie and thank him.

SHE FOUND HIM in the booth with Grady.

"There's quite a crowd in the lobby," Charlie was

telling him. "Anything I can do? Whatever you want, you got it."

"Nope." Grady leaned back in his chair, Sam on his lap happily chewing on the sleeve of Grady's sweatshirt. "I've got ten minutes of Hildegarde of Bingen on now, and then I'll say my goodbyes and go to jail."

"Oh, Grady," Allie sat down on the floor of the booth. "I still wish you hadn't said anything. We could have—"

"No, this is going to be great." Grady's voice sounded so self-satisfied that Allie jerked her head up to see if he could possibly be that happy.

He was.

"This is exactly the forum we need," Grady told her. "We need to get this stuff legalized for medical treatment. Now we have a cause. They're going to have to arrest me and my mother and probably a half-dozen cancer patients. Think of the publicity when Mrs. Winthrop goes to jail. Your celibate bet made the tri-state news. This will have to go national."

Allie went back to the part that scared her the most. "Grady, you're going to jail."

Grady grinned at her. "Not for long. You don't know my dad. Hell, *I* didn't know my dad. He yelled at first, but he had a plan worked out, and then Mom got on the other line, and by the time she was finished, he was ready to run me for governor. He's all gung ho, getting lawyers and filing motions and calling the press. He says there's bail and appeals and no end of lawyer red tape he can throw at them to keep me out. And the whole time, Mom and I will be giving interviews, making statements..." He trailed off as his grin widened. "I bet Dad will even let me keep my show once he gets over the shock."

"He's over it now," Charlie told him from where he was leaning on the side of the booth. "He's arguing with the sheriff in front of the TV cameras. This is going to be a circus."

Grady leaned back in his chair. "This is great."

Allie stood up, suddenly reassured. "No, it's not, but I'll help, anyway." She started out of the booth, and Charlie caught her arm.

"What are you doing?"

Allie smiled at him, buoyed by Grady's optimism and the fact that Charlie was touching her again. "You know all those people I was going to call to try to stop your drug story? They work both ways. I'll have Grady on the national news by tomorrow."

"Oh, right," Charlie snorted. "Even you—"

Allie stopped him in midsentence. "Want to bet?"

"No." Charlie shook his head. "Absolutely not. I'm not betting anything with you ever again."

"That's what I thought," Allie said and left the booth to make some phone calls.

THREE HOURS LATER, Grady had been arrested and bailed out, and Charlie was alone with Bill in his office.

"Things didn't turn out quite the way I'd planned," Charlie told him.

Bill sighed and sat heavily in his chair. "The two of them. Running a charity drug ring. And now they're in hog heaven, and the poor old sheriff has to go through the motions. If they'd kept their damn mouths shut…"

"At least now you know," Charlie said. "The anonymous-letter mystery's over."

"Oh, yeah, I'm real glad about that." Bill leaned back in his chair and glared at him. "So I guess this means you're leaving."

"Nope," Charlie said. "I'm staying. You can tell my dad he won."

Bill started and then tried to look innocent. "What's your dad got to do with this?"

Charlie shook his head. "Forget it. I figured it out a while back. You called Dad and told him you had an anonymous letter, and he told him he wanted me settled down and you cooked this up together. Favor for an old friend, right? You didn't give a damn about that letter."

"I told him I couldn't make you stay if you didn't want to." Bill scowled at him. "Then you went and made yourself a hit. And me some money. It's your fault."

"No, it's Allie's." Charlie sighed. "She wanted to make me a star."

"Well, I got to tell you, son, I'm real glad she did."

Charlie looked up in surprise at the emotion in the older man's voice. "I am, too." He blinked at the thought. He really was glad.

That's what hanging around with Allie had done for him. Made him career crazy.

"You're sure gonna make the nights interesting around here," Bill went on, and Charlie shook his head.

"No, that'll be the mornings. I want the drive-time spot."

Bill frowned at him. "Can't do it. That's Mark King's show."

Charlie shrugged. "Then I'm out of here. And so is Allie."

Bill's eyebrows shot up. "Alice? She's not leaving."

"We're getting married, Bill. Whither I goest, she goest. And if we don't get the drive-time show, we're going." Charlie mentally crossed his fingers, hoping Bill wouldn't call his bluff. Allie was too independent to follow anybody anywhere, but Bill didn't have to know that.

Bill glared at him. "What the hell am I going to do with Mark?"

"I am not the person to ask that," Charlie said as he stood up. "You wouldn't like my suggestions."

"All right." Bill ground his teeth a little. "All right. You got it."

"Thank you very much." Charlie turned back as he got to the door. "And good luck with Grady and Beattie. Let me know if there's anything I can do."

Bill sat back in his chair. "We can handle it. It's a family problem."

Charlie leaned in the doorway. "Well, to tell you the truth, Bill, I kind of think of you and Grady and Beattie as family now. So if you need anything…"

Bill's face softened and he nodded. "I'll call you."

"Thanks. I'd like that."

Charlie looked in Allie's office, but she was long gone, her phone calls made while he was helping Grady.

He knew where she'd be, and he tried not to think about it on his way out to the car.

Now was no time to have a heart attack from lust.

ALLIE OPENED the door of her apartment when he knocked, and just the sight of him made her weak-kneed. Coming home to bed had been a mistake. It was November first, and Grady was where he wanted to be, and the bet was over, and she wanted him. She didn't want to lose the closeness they'd had, but she wanted him with a craving that went beyond lust.

So when she opened the door, and he was standing there, broad and safe and male and Charlie, her knees went, and she tried to pretend it didn't matter. "Come on in," she said and then went back into her bedroom and crawled under her quilt. "I can't believe this," she told him when he followed her. "I can't believe this last twenty-four hours happened. I can't believe this last *month* happened."

Charlie slumped at the foot of the bed, and Allie fought back her disappointment. He was supposed to be under the quilt with her.

"It happened," he told her. "The last thing I heard as I went through the lobby was Mark, on the air, telling the world he'd inhaled in the seventies."

Allie was so surprised, she forgot to lust for a minute. "Inhaled what?"

"I don't know." Charlie rubbed his neck. "I don't care. I'm just glad it's over. I just want some sleep."

Sleep. Well, it was a start. She moved over a couple of inches to make room for him. "You can get some sleep here if you want."

He was still for a moment. "Here?"

She nodded.

"Allie, if I climb into bed with you, I'm going to want more than sleep."

Her heart did a little heated lurch in her chest. *Thank God.* Now, if only things didn't change. "I've been thinking," she said to him. "All last night, and this morning while I was on the phone. And I don't know what I think about this Grady mess. I don't even know which one of us is right. But I do know that you did what you thought was right even though I tried hard to change your mind." She smiled tentatively at him. "And I'm pretty impressed with that, that you'd give up everything to do what you thought was right. And I know that you've been right on some other things this month, too. Not everything, but some things. And I know I love you, and you love me, and after that…well, I think we can work this out." She swallowed. "What do you think?"

Charlie's eyes met hers. "Will you marry me?"

Allie almost fell out of bed.

"I already told Bill we were getting married, so I'm going to look like a real fool if you say no." He leaned forward. "Make an honest man out of me. Marry me."

Allie stopped breathing. Marriage. That was permanent enough. And since it was Charlie asking, it was forever. She'd have to follow him all over the country, and they'd probably have all their kids in different states, and she'd never have a career again.

But she'd have good times. And laughter.

And Charlie.

She drew a deep breath. "Can we get a Winnebago?"

He blinked at her. "Well, yeah. Sure. I guess." He frowned at her. "Why would you want a Winnebago?"

"So it'll be like home while we're traveling," Allie said. "Like a house."

Charlie's frown deepened. "Traveling where?"

"Wherever it is that we're going. It's November."

He started to laugh, and she wanted to kill him. "Forget the Winnebago. We're not going anywhere. I told Bill I wanted a full-time job. Medical insurance. Pension plan. Paternity leave. We're adopting Sam. I'm settling down."

Some days, you get everything you ask for. Unbelievable. Allie sank back against the pillows. "Oh. Oh, good." She closed her eyes in relieved wonder. "Oh, Charlie, I do love you, and I'd follow you anywhere, but I'd really rather—"

"Stay here and make me a star." Charlie grinned at her. "I know, babe. You've got it."

Allie loved him so much she thought she'd die of it. And he was still a whole bed-length away from her. She tried to glare at him. "Will you please come here and kiss me? You just proposed. You're supposed to kiss me."

His grin disappeared. "I'm not going to stop with a kiss. I want a lot more than that."

Allie took a deep breath. "You've got it."

His eyes met hers and he didn't move. "This is unbelievable," he told her. "I feel like a kid on a first date."

"It's not like we haven't done this before." Allie tried to smile at him. "It's not like it's our first time."

"Yes, it is." Charlie moved up until he was sitting on the side of the bed, his hands on each side of her, and she put her hand on his arm, grateful to finally be touching him. "It's our first time for this," he said, his eyes looking deep into hers. "What we had before was fun, but it wasn't this. This is our first time."

She couldn't move her eyes from his. "I know." She moved her hand to his cheek, barely touching him. "I know. I want you so much. I couldn't bear to lose you now."

She hadn't meant to sound so vulnerable, but she couldn't call back the words. He closed his eyes, and then he shook his head. "You won't lose me. Things have changed, but they'll be better. They're already better. If you don't want to move this fast, we can wait to make love. Until you're sure."

"I'm sure," Allie said. "I'm just…nervous."

"I know. I am, too. But I want you so much…"

He leaned forward then and kissed her softly, lingering, and the heat from his mouth went straight into her bones and called back all the cravings she'd ignored for too long.

"Oh, come to bed," she whispered. "I can't wait any longer."

He stood then and undressed, deliberately, not like the old exuberant Charlie who had stripped at the speed of light and then pulled her to him like a teenager in heat. When he slid into bed beside her, he didn't touch her; he just supported himself on one elbow and looked down at her as if she was something irreplaceable.

"This must be what wedding nights used to be like," he said. "Terrifying. Incredible."

Allie put her hand on his chest to feel his warmth and felt him stiffen at her touch. She'd forgotten exactly how good he could feel under her hand, how hard his chest was, how hot his skin burned, like a brand on her palm. She let her hand trail down his chest and put her cheek against him and listened to his heart pound, and he slowly slid his arm around her waist and pulled her close as he eased himself under her, onto the pillows.

Charlie tipped her face to his, and she almost suffocated from love, just watching him look at her as if he was memorizing her. There was so much love in his face, she thought she'd drown in it, and when he finally did pull her head down to kiss her, she did drown. His mouth was gentle at first, and then more insistent, his tongue invading her, and her hands clenched his shoulders as he grew more demanding. She felt her body deepen in heat against his, her blood growing thick and hot as his mouth took her away, and she willed herself to remember that it was him with her and not to melt into senselessness. She felt him pull at her nightgown and helped him strip it off, closing her eyes as the cool air fell on her body, opening them as the heat from his hands reclaimed her. She licked at the base of his neck, and then down his chest to his nipples, feeling how hard and smooth he was under her lips, hearing his breathing break as she touched him.

Then he bent his head, and she felt the sweet chill of his mouth on her breast, and then the chill turned to heat. She raked her fingers through his hair and pulled his head against her, savoring the ache of his mouth on her. The heat and the ache and the torment were everywhere, and as he moved under her, she fell into him, becoming part of him, wanting him everywhere against her, inside her. Even simple pleasures like the brush of his cheek against her skin became charged with electricity and love.

"I love you," she whispered to him, and he said, "I didn't know this existed. I didn't know until you."

"Make love to me." Allie tried to move against him, but he rolled her gently onto her back and began to kiss her neck. "I want you inside me," she said, arching into him. "I've waited so long. Don't make me wait longer."

"Just a little bit," he said against her throat. "Just a little bit." His cheek was on her breast and then his tongue traced down the seam of her stomach, and her nerves fluttered and she forgot how to breathe.

"Soon," he said, when his hands were on her hips, and her hips flexed on their own, tightening under his grip. "I just need to taste you. I need this first." His fingers found her, and she moaned and stretched to ease the ache, then he licked his tongue inside her, and she jerked under the shock and grabbed the headboard above her in desperation, holding on to it as if it were sanity.

"You taste so sweet, Allie," she heard him whisper, and she moaned at the thought while his breath tantalized her thighs. She gripped the headboard until her knuckles went white, trying to stay with him, but his whisper pounded inside her and she couldn't breathe because the heat was everywhere. "You're so sweet."

And then he licked inside her again and again, and she writhed in his grasp, and he moved his mouth harder against her, holding her hips harder against him, and she couldn't twist away, didn't want to twist away, had to twist away as the heat screamed through her veins until she cried out, "Oh, Charlie, *now*," and he whispered, "Soon," and drove her on and on until she went over the edge, ecstatically out of control.

He moved back beside her then while she throbbed against him and the aftershocks of her climax wracked her. He whispered that she was beautiful, most beautiful when she was coming, and she breathed, "It's not enough. I need you inside me." And he closed his eyes and then moved over her, his lips saying her name soundlessly, his thighs moving her legs apart. She ached so for him that she moaned with it, her veins bursting under her skin. "Oh, please," she said, clutching him to her, and he said, "Look at me," and when she did, loving him so much she was insane with it, drowning in the heat and love she saw in his eyes, he moved into her, filling her, and they both stopped breathing for that moment, their eyes locked on each other, their bodies tensed together as the shock flooded them both.

And then they moved together, breathed together, and the heat rushed through them, and Allie surged and bloomed, feeling Charlie in her fingertips, in her heart, in her brain, as his warmth and light and love moved through her, and she fell into her climax, screaming with it, feeling him surge against her over and over, beyond measured rhythm, and his shuddering moans brought her back into the aching spiral again and again until she thought she'd die of ecstasy.

And when they were both quiet, both breathing again, holding each other in the early-morning sunlight, Charlie kissed her and said, "I love you, Allie. I'll never stop loving you."

She nodded against his cheek, weak with spent passion. "I know. This is forever."

She felt him relax, and then moments later he was asleep in her arms, and she held him tightly until she fell asleep, too.

IT WAS AFTERNOON when she woke up, and Charlie woke, too, when she stirred. He pulled her close and she closed her eyes when he kissed her forehead. "I forgot to tell you the good news," he whispered. "We've got a new show."

Allie frowned at him, still half-asleep. "What new show?"

"Bill gave us the drive-time spot," he murmured into her hair. "The one at 6:00 a.m. You're back where you wanted to be."

Allie sat up, suddenly awake and appalled. "Did you say 6:00 a.m.? In the morning a.m.? Are you nuts?"

Charlie blinked and pushed himself up beside her on one arm. "I thought that was what you wanted. Back on top."

Allie looked exasperated. "I can be on top at night."

He grinned at her and moved his hand to her breast and said, "Anytime," and she grinned, too, covering his hand with hers. "You know what I mean," she told him. "I like the ten-to-two people. They're bizarre. Let Mark have the drive-time show. At least until Marcia takes it away from him, which should be any day now. We belong at night, Charlie." She looked at him anxiously. "Don't you think so?"

"Well, yes." Charlie started to laugh and collapsed

back into the bed, pulling her on top of him. "Wait'll
I tell Bill."

Allie propped herself up on his chest, enjoying the
way her breasts squashed against him. "I can't believe
you even considered the morning show."

Charlie sighed. "I thought I was giving you what
you wanted."

"You always give me what I want. Which reminds
me…" Allie moved her face to his until they were
nose-to-nose, stretching and feeling the long hard
length of his body against hers. He'd be hers for the
rest of her life. She almost died just thinking about it.
Then his hand moved lazily down her back to her rear
end, and she brought her mind back to the subject at
hand. "I have an idea for a new show," Allie told
him. "It'll run forever. Audience of one. I'm thinking
of calling it Charlie All Afternoon. And the playlist—"

"I do my own playlist," Charlie told her and kissed
her to start the program.

A GREAT READ
GUARANTEED

We are so confident that you will love this book that we are offering a 100% money-back guarantee!*

If you are not satisfied for whatever reason MIRA® Books** will refund the amount you have paid (as shown on receipt) in full. Simply fill in the form below and send us a **copy of your receipt**, along with a stamped, self-addressed envelope to*:

**MIRA® Guaranteed Read,
PO Box 676, Richmond, Surrey TW9 1WU**

A GREAT READ GUARANTEED   CAN

Please send this form with a copy of your receipt and a stamped, self-addressed envelope to the address above. We will send you a cheque for the purchase price of the book within 4-6 weeks.

If you didn't enjoy this book, we'd really like to know why!

The book was not what I was expecting   ❑

The storyline did not hold my interest   ❑

I did not enjoy the characters   ❑

I did not think the book was good value for money   ❑

If you would like to give us more information, or if you have another reason, please let us know here:

_____

_____

MIRA®
An international collection of bestselling authors

EVER AFTER
by *Fiona Hood-Stewart*

"An enthralling page turner—
not to be missed." —*New York Times*
bestselling author Joan Johnston

**She belongs to a world of wealth,
politics and social climbing. But
now Elm must break away to find
happily ever after...**

Elm MacBride can no longer sit back and
watch her corrupt and deceitful husband's
ascent to power and his final betrayal sends her
fleeing to Switzerland where she meets
Irishman Johnny Graney. When her husband's
actions threaten to destroy her, Johnny must
save not only their love but Elm's life...

ISBN 07783 2078 2

Published 15th April 2005